Geek Merit Badges

Geek Merit Badges

ESSENTIAL SKILLS FOR NERDY EXCELLENCE

MEGHAN MURPHY

Cincinnati, Ohio
www.howdesign.com

 Published by HOW Books, an imprint of F+W, a Content + Ecommerce Company, 10151 Carver Road, Suite 200, Blue Ash, Ohio 45242. (800) 289-0963. First edition.

For more excellent books and resources for designers, visit www.howdesign.com.

19 18 17 16 15   5 4 3 2 1

ISBN-13: 978-1-4403-3676-8

Distributed in Canada by Fraser Direct
100 Armstrong Avenue
Georgetown, Ontario, Canada L7G 5S4
Tel: (905) 877-4411

Distributed in the U.K. and Europe by F&W Media International, LTD
Brunel House, Forde Close, Newton Abbot, TQ12 4PU, UK
Tel: (+44) 1626 323200, Fax: (+44) 1626 323319
Email: enquiries@fwmedia.com

Distributed in Australia by Capricorn Link
P.O. Box 704, Windsor, NSW 2756 Australia
Tel: (02) 4560-1600

Edited by Scott Francis
Illustrations by Meghan Murphy
Designed by Claudean Wheeler
Production coordinated by Greg Nock

Dedication

This is for all my follow dreamers, space cadets, weirdos and odd ducks. Stay strong and proud, and be the geek you want to see in the world.

Acknowledgments

Thanks to my family for letting me be geeky.

Thanks to my friends for being geekier.

And thanks to all the geekery still out there waiting to be discovered.

CONTENTS

ABSORPTION MERIT BADGES

TRANSMISSION MERIT BADGES

CREATION MERIT BADGES

BADGE TRACKERS

INTRODUCTION

How do you know you are a geek? Is there a quiz you have to take? Or is it more like a checklist of symptoms? Is it the way you look, the way you dress, the way others decide to see you?

That's not how it works, but in your heart you already know that.

You are a geek because you are a geek. You love what you love; your passions are rich, and you aren't embarrassed to be yourself. But of course, since you're a geek you want to be the best geek you can be—and this is where the Geek Merit Badges come in!

This book is for anyone who wants to do more stuff, try new things, and remember how great being excited can truly be. Plus there are badges to collect! Hoorah!

Geek: Defined

What does this book mean by the term *geek*? For our purposes it is simply anyone who loves science fiction, fantasy, movies, television shows, comics, anime, toys, games, or anything else in the pop culture atmosphere that at one time or another has been labeled "uncool" or "nerdy." A geek is anyone whose love is deep and unashamed.

Of course, there are plenty of other more restrictive definitions of *geek* (and finer tunings of the related terms *nerd* and *dork*), but this isn't a scholastic paper or a link-bait article. We divide ourselves too much as it is.

The Geek Merit Badges aren't a test of geekiness but rather a celebration of it. Enjoy!

How to Use This Guide

This book is designed to help you explore and discover all (or at least a sizeable chunk of) the facets of your inner and outer geek. To make navigation easier, the Geek Merit Badges are divided into four categories: Discovery, Absorption, Transmission and Creation. Taken together, these four areas cover a large swath of possible life geekery.

- The **Discovery** badges address your geeky beginnings.
- The **Absorption** badges are all about what motivates and excites you.
- The **Transmission** badges delve into the myriad ways you can share your enthusiasm.
- And the **Creation** badges showcase all the incredible things your geekiness can inspire you to make.

Follow along, have fun, and enjoy all the ways that being a geek is fantastic.

The Good Geek Code

A Good Geek:

- is always ready for an adventure.
- is never bored.
- shares the awesome freely.
- loves the best (and the rest).
- has a zero asshole policy.
- has no regrets (mostly).
- Most of all, a Good Geek knows that the things that make a person a geek are the very same things that make a person amazing.

DISCOVERY MERIT BADGES

You wake up one day and you are a geek. No, wait, that's not quite true, is it? You aren't born with passion: You discover it. It's like a gift the universe gives to you. "Here," it says, "Check out all this amazing stuff. Dive in, my friend." You are a geek because you heard the call. Congratulations! Not everyone is lucky enough to be picked for team geekery. Poor bastards. Living without passion must be like only seeing a rainbow in gray.

The Discovery badges are all about your beginnings. Those things that got you started, and still get you excited. You know, the good stuff.

This section features badges to help you celebrate your beginnings, and all the ideas and the inspirations that started your geek life.

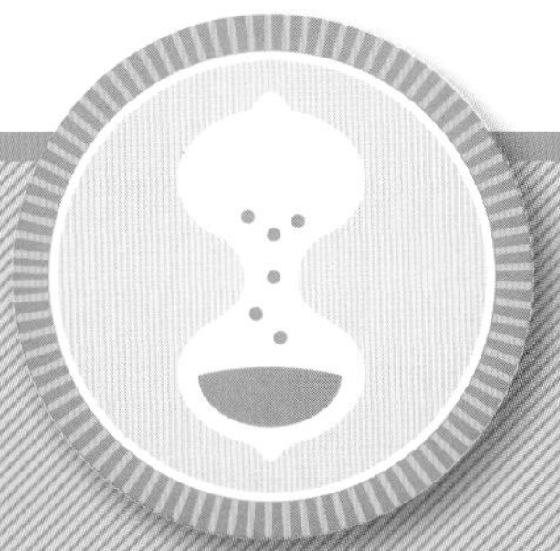

Time and Time Again Badge

"No matter where you go, there you are."

Time travel. You've read the books, seen the movies. You know it's a horrible idea. But it is so tempting, right? Not just the idea of changing History-with-a-big-H, but changing your own history, fixing your own mistakes. A larger-than-we'd-like part of the geek collective memory is taken up with embarrassment and mistakes that sure would be nice to replace with some triumphant memories. But time travel is just another way to live in the past, and we've always had our eyes on the future. Time travel: Fun to imagine, kind of a drag to live.

WHO SAID THAT? Each merit badge features a relevant quote. Test your personal knowledge and see if you can correctly identify the quote. (Or just cheat and skip to the answers in the Badge Trackers section on page 153.)

Time Travel Possibilities

There's more than one way to meddle in the past! What's your poison?

machine

magic

lesson-teaching ghosts

wormhole

travel into own younger/ older self's consciousness

general timey-wimey stuff

Reasons for Time Travel

There are some very noble—and even more not-so-noble—motivations to mess with the space-time continuum. Here is a sample list, ranked from best to worst.

- Save universe from total destruction.
- Save the Earth from total destruction.
- Save [insert important, and hopefully benevolent, historical figure here].
- Buy that winning lotto ticket.

- Change a test score.
- Not eat that second slice of pie.
- 'Cause it seemed like a good idea at the time.

Paradox Avoidance Chart

Don't suffer from I'm-My-Own-Grandparent Syndrome.

RIGHT:

Your Timeline

Your Parents' Timeline

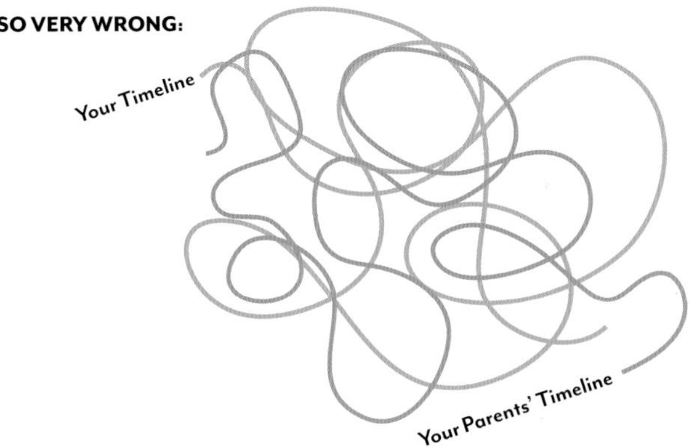

Your Personal Time Travel Plan

If you were to go back in time, the two things you'd probably want to ask yourself before changing anything would be 1) *Could I*? and 2) *Should I*? If you step on the wrong butterfly, all of a sudden the world is up to its eyeballs in alien invaders and you never get that promotion. So plan ahead with this exercise.

AN EMBARRASSING MOMENT OF YOUR LIFE:

Could you change it? **Y** or **N**

Should you change it? **Y** or **N**

If you answered **Y** to both: How would you change it?

....

....

....

....

A SCARY MOMENT OF YOUR LIFE:

Could you change it? **Y** or **N**

Should you change it? **Y** or **N**

If you answered **Y** to both: How would you change it?

....

....

....

....

A TOUGH MOMENT OF YOUR LIFE:

Could you change it? **Y** or **N**

Should you change it? **Y** or **N**

If you answered **Y** to both: How would you change it?

....

....

....

....

A WEIRD MOMENT OF YOUR LIFE:

Could you change it? **Y** or **N**

Should you change it? **Y** or **N**

If you answered **Y** to both: How would you change it?

....

....

....

....

A HAPPY MOMENT OF YOUR LIFE:

Could you change it? **Y** or **N**

Should you change it? **Y** or **N**

If you answered **Y** to both: How would you change it?

....

....

....

....

A LIFE-CHANGING MOMENT OF YOUR LIFE (KNOWN AS *THE REVERSE CHANGE*):

Could you change it? **Y** or **N**

Should you change it? **Y** or **N**

If you answered **Y** to both: How would you change it?

....

....

....

....

Awkwardness Adept Badge

"I, myself, am strange and unusual."

Odd. Weird. Doesn't quite fit in. These traits turn out to be the best training in potential awesomeness that you could ever have. Geeks don't fear the awkward like most people: We live it; we embrace it; we swim in the warm waters of what-the-hell. When you aren't worried about not fitting in, you get really good at standing out.

Awkward Level Check

Also known as "Things I Find To Be More Difficult Than They Should Be"

unexpected phone calls (*What are we? Animals?*)

eye contact (*That's a good way to lose a soul.*)

small talk (*If only it were microscopic talk.*)

dressing self (*There must be more holes than buttons on this shirt.*)

awareness of surroundings (*I swear that window was a door before.*)

too many people (*Don't pop my personal space bubble!*)

Helpful Eye Contact Chart

How much is too much? It's good to know before you start.

The Art of Artlessness: Being Purposefully Awkward

To get comfortable with anything, particularly your own skin, sometimes you have to turn everything up to eleven. This activity is all about sinking right up to your neck in oddness until it starts to feel like home. The key is to act with courage and clarity of purpose.

- Mismatch your socks.
- Dance when you know everyone's watching.
- Stand in the middle of the elevator.
- Don't hate at least one photo of yourself.
- Sing karaoke without regret.

Comrades in Arms Badge

"I have been—and always shall be—your friend."

Build and cultivate your team. You've got to have people with whom to create, explore and execute elaborate shenanigans (someone has to hold the flashlight!). There are thousands of two-to-infinity person adventures that are waiting to be conquered by you and your party. They are the ones you can trust, and the ones who can trust you. It can be dangerous out there. Don't go alone.

Ways to Describe a Geektastic Relationship

How do you get along with your fellow geeks? If you can't find the right words, try some of these.

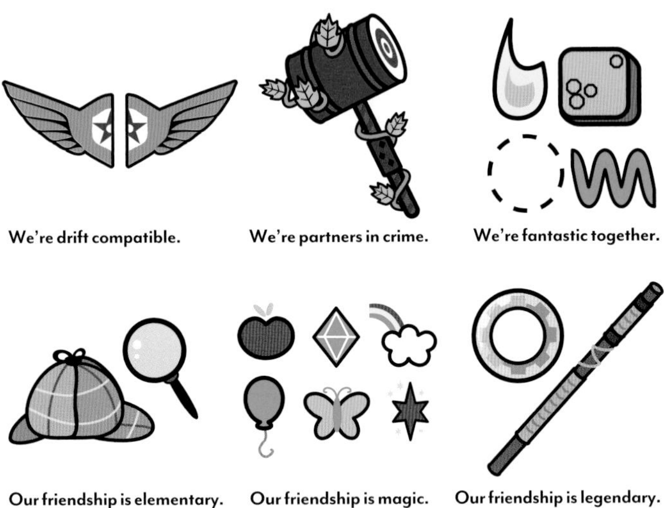

We're drift compatible.

We're partners in crime.

We're fantastic together.

Our friendship is elementary.

Our friendship is magic.

Our friendship is legendary.

Possible Interactions Database

Feel a little stale in your relationships? Do you wonder if maybe you're not experiencing the full range of human interactions? Want to maximize your networking possibilites? See how many options you can cross off your encounters list.

- neighbor that you wave to
- neighbor you definitely don't wave to
- school chum
- colleague

- acquaintance
- more-than-acquaintance-but-not-quite-friend
- friend
- best friend
- partner
- enemy
- frenemy
- future enemy

Build Your Party

Every adventuring party needs to be well rounded in order to survive the horrors of a deadly dungeon, and unfortunately, "horrors of a deadly dungeon" can be the perfect description of everyday life at times. So it is a smart plan to know your friends' abilities and powers, and know who can fit the following classic roles when snarling monsters stand between you and your goals.

The Fighter:
Tough. Strong. Takes not an ounce of crap from anyone. Stands up for the weak. Never gets shortchanged. Has a giant, gooey heart underneath.

The Healer:
Comforting. Robust. The rock. Is always there with open ear and open arms. Has a vast reserve of patience and respect. Can cure anything from hangovers to heartbreaks.

The Magic User:
Smart. Mysterious. Always reading something. Has answers to questions you didn't know you had. Often quiet—unless conveying knowledge on rare/odd/arcane subjects.

The Rogue:
Quick. Clever. The tricky one. Generally up to something. Knows how to get out of a sticky situation. Has trouble seeing the difference between fun and trouble sometimes.

*Note: In life, just as in a game, there are times when you and your friends need to reroll your characters. Identifying your strengths and abilities is not be the same as being restricted by them. Sometimes the fighter needs to cast her own magic, and sometimes the healer has to kick a little ass.

Health Bar Awareness Badge

"The spice must flow."

There are some pitfalls to the geek way, and many of them involve the fact that we are mere fragile bags of flesh (at least for now), with all the weaknesses inherent in living the mortal life. A good geek must stay in tune with his or her body and mind, and keep them humming along with regular checks and maintenance. Be good to yourself, you deserve it.

Ways Your Geekery Will Try to Kill You

Do any of these maddening siren calls sounds familiar?

- Just one more episode
- Just one more level
- Just one more chapter
- Just one more revision
- Just one more quarter
- Just one more round
- Just one more roll
- Just one more hour

Beware These Geek-Specific Ailments!

Have you ever suffered from:

- Reboot Rage
- Pull List Panic
- Kaiju Kramps
- Extended Universe-itus
- Sudden Onset Slash Syndrome
- Midnight Movie Madness
- Next-Gen Console Complex
- Final-Book-In-Series Publication Paranoia (related: Trilogy Expansion Disorder)

Is This All-Nighter Worth It?

Sleeping. Sometimes it can seem like such a waste of time when there are so many things you want to do. The world is finally quiet, and it has left you the keys to the night. But you know you will pay for it in the morning, when the sun blazes down on you in judgment, and your body stops taking your calls. So use this space to write down pros and cons to consult the next time all night seems right. Hopefully you'll be equipped to make an informed choice. No guarantees, though.

Pros

....

....

....

....

....

Cons

....

....

....

....

....

Count the pros, subtract the cons. Do the math!

Self-Destruct Override Sequence

Pack your very own self-care kit and be prepared for any sick/lame/bummer days. Don't let the bastards grind you down.

Culture Code Badge

"I find your lack of faith disturbing."

As a geek, your sense of the world comes from the stories you've heard. The logic of Spock. The cleverness of Hermione. The ass kicking of Ripley. The bravery of Frodo (with an assist from the sheer tenacity—and upper body strength—of Samwise.) What you've watched and read and absorbed through hungry osmosis has taken deep root in your heart. Your geekery has made you a better person.

HOW TO WATCH A TWILIGHT ZONE MARATHON

Maybe it's the beginning of a new year and you want to start fresh. Maybe you need a little top off of the old morality tank. Or maybe you just really like Jack Klugman. All of these and more are fantastic reasons for digesting a chunk of *Twilight Zone* episodes. Here are some handy tips to keep you alert, safe and (relatively) sane.

- Remember to look outside occasionally to remind yourself the bomb hasn't dropped, aliens haven't landed, and the world isn't slowly becoming unbearably hot (or in actuality unbearably cold).
- Alternate heavy episodes with maybe-a-tiny-bit-of-humanity-isn't-a-festering-pile-of-rot episodes.
- If you start hearing your own thoughts in Rod Serling's staccato narration, it's time to take a break.
- Keep an extra pair of glasses handy. Just in case.

Geeky Choices

Use the following checklist to see how geek-tuned your life compass is.

Have you ever:

- ❑ based a major life decision on a similar situation from a book, movie or television show?

- ❑ chosen a romantic partner because he or she reminded you of a favorite fictional character? And did you ever tell them?
- ❑ named a computer, pet or child based on your favorite book, movie or television show?
- ❑ chosen a college major/career path inspired by a book, movie or television show?
- ❑ made the right choice because the wrong choice would have disappointed your favorite character?
- ❑ imagined yourself as a favorite character and did more than you thought you could?
- ❑ conquered a fear using your favorite geeky thing as a reward?

Geeky Life Mottos (And Their Meanings)

- **Live long and prosper.** *Try not to die too young or too poor.*
- **I ain't got time to bleed.** *I have both poor first aid and time management skills.*
- **Don't panic.** *Don't panic. Unless it is clearly time to panic, and then go totally bugnuts.*
- **May the Force be with you.** *Be safe and well. Or, I hope you are filled with tiny little nonsense creatures.*
- **Why so serious?** *The meaning of this motto really depends on your mental state and amount of misapplied lipstick.*

- **I am a leaf on the wind. Watch how I soar.** *I am one with the world. Until the world wants to kill me.*
- **Fear is the mind-killer.** *Being afraid can stop you from achieving greatness. Of course, it can also stop you from severely hurting or killing yourself, so try to be moderate in your fear avoidance.*
- **Knowing is half the battle.** *The other half is mostly paperwork.*

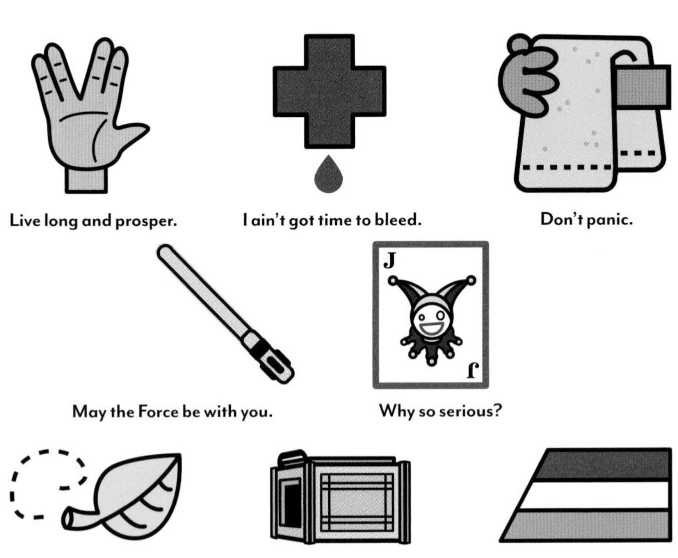

Live long and prosper.

I ain't got time to bleed.

Don't panic.

May the Force be with you.

Why so serious?

I am a leaf on the wind.

Fear is the mind-killer.

Knowing is half the battle.

What Did We Learn Today?

Write down the top five lessons living the geek life has taught you.

1. ....
2. ....
3. ....
4. ....
5. ....

Your Own Worst Enemy Badge

"Good. Bad. I'm the guy with the gun."

Your evil twin: It's either a metaphor for fighting our own worst impulses or that actual alternate universe bastard that has been gunning for you. What better way to know yourself than to learn to recognize and understand who you are when you are not you—or to be ready for that final boss battle where the bad guy turns out to be yourself.

Evil Twin Signs

Keep an eye out for these classic signs of up-to-no-good-ness.

goatee

scar (somewhere badass)

arched eyebrow

***mwahaha* laugh**

everything is extra pointy (teeth, ears, hair, etc.)

fifty percent less clothing (and 100% more gold lame)

Evil Twin Spotting

There are a myriad of types of other yous out there. As you see them out in the world—most likely lurking on the edges of your life, waiting for the perfect moment to strike—check them off.

- alternative/darkest timeline duplicate
- clone
- shadow self
- escaped mirror version

- separated-at-birth twin seeking revenge
- sexy vampire version
- pod person
- advanced robot
- your own deepest insecurities made flesh

Fail-Safe Questions

Have these safety questions filled out and kept in a secure location so your friends can tell who is who when the inevitable and super dramatic rooftop showdown happens. (Make a copy of this list and hide it. I mean it. You'll regret it if you don't.)

What is your greatest weakness?

....

What is the source of your power?

....

What is the most precious thing in the world to you?

....

Where do you hide all your secrets?

....

What's something only you would know?

....

If *You Are* the Evil Twin.

Everything you need is right here. *Mwahahahaha!*

Call to Adventure Badge

> *"Roads? Where we're going we don't need roads."*

You didn't choose the geek life; the geek life chose you. One day you put down your ever-present book, laid down your trusty controller, and stopped drawing your favorite dinosaur for a second as the realization slowly but surely dawned: *I'm a geek. I love geeky things, and I'm ready for whatever adventure the geek path has along its way. Excelsior!*

My Geeky Firsts

It's important to remember and commemorate your beginnings. Celebrate those tiny seeds that sprouted in your brain and grew into the wonderfully weird network of passions and experiences that made you, you.

My first Saturday morning cartoon:

....

My first late-night movie:

....

My first nerdy shirt:

....

My first gadget:

....

My first fictional crush:

....

My first trilogy:

....

My first surprise ending:

....

My first devastating cancellation:

....

My first medically required social stigma (glasses/braces/inhaler):

....

My first geek-powered success:

....

Life Cycle of a Geeky Love

Refer to the following chart whenever you are unsure of where you are in the typical progression of obsession.

"This looks interesting." "I might kinda like this." "I'm in love." "Gimme! Gimme! Gimme!"

Scouting Ahead

The call of the geek is not a one-time thing. The invitation to a new favorite is always just around the bend. But this also means you can't be complacent and wait for it to come to you. Take some initiative and seek out that televison series you've been hearing about, a film by that director everyone says you'll love, or that board game that intimidates you a little.

Write down at least one new choice in each category and then check it off once you've experienced it.

Movie:

....

Television series (at least 3 episodes):

....

Cartoon (at least 3 episodes):

....

Book:

....

Comic:

....

Food:

....

Convention:

....

Game (console or computer):

....

Game (board or card):

....

Origin Story Badge

"With great power comes great responsibility."

You are the hero (or villain, depending on personal preference) of your own story. Geeks specialize in seeking out and absorbing the greatest of tales, creating an individually curated mental library from which to choose all the best parts. Be your own bard! Write your own legend!

A Collection of Possible Origins

"I was born." *Hmm... That needs a little jazzing up.* Try adding one (or more) of the classic origins to spice things up.

A Repository of Creation

Use these categories to gather and sort different origin stories you've enjoyed in your geeky studies. You never know when you'll need a good beginning.

TRAUMATIC STARTS

(example: Harry Potter)

....

....

....

....

....

CALLED BY DESTINY

(example: Buffy Summers)

....

....

....

....

....

GOOD LUCK/BAD LUCK

(example: The Fantastic Four)

....

....

....

....

....

The Me. The Myth. The Legend.

Fill in the blanks to get started on creating your own story. Be creative—it's all up to you!

I discovered my path in life when ....

....

My special power is...

and it comes from ....

I fight for .... ,

.... ,

and ....

I protect ....

My ultimate goal is ....

If you want to be my enemy, all you have to do is ....

....

I look for ....

and .... in a sidekick.

I always win because I ....

Joined the Party Badge

"It's alive!"

The alpha fandom: a geek's first love. That one book, movie, television show or comic that started it all. It's that flutter in your chest, that rush of sweet chemicals to your brain that makes you blush and stumble and feel alive. Even as you grow, move on and discover new obsessions, you will always have a special place of honor for that initial spark that jump-started your geek heartbeat.

My First Fandom

Fill in the blanks to create a record of your inaugural come-to-geek experience.

My first fandom was:

....

I discovered it when:

....

I knew I was hooked when:

....

It was important to me because:

....

My most precious fan-related item was:

....

The longest I was ever engaged in a fan activity was:

....

My most triumphant fan moment was:

....

My most embarrassing fan moment was:

....

My absolute proudest fan moment was:

....

I will always love my first fandom because:

....

Assorted Relevant Charts

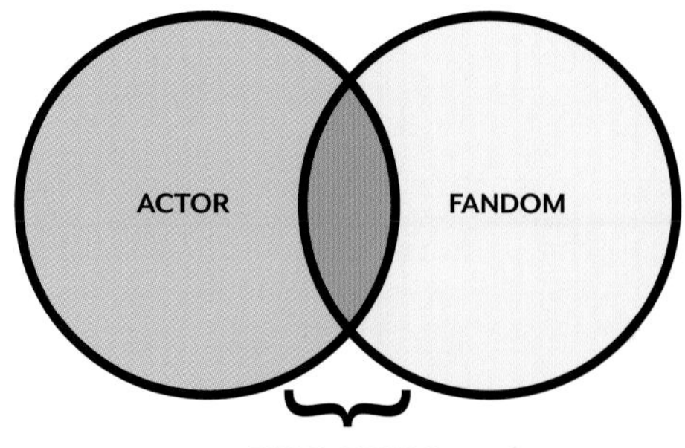

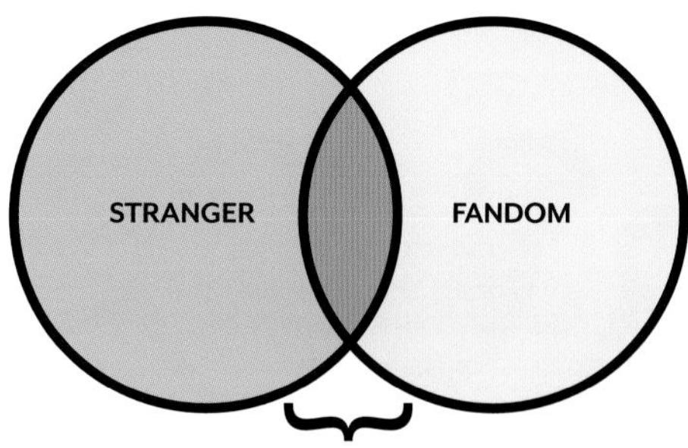

My First Fan Portait

Use the blank form to draw how you looked when you first found your true geek self: your first television show– or movie-themed shirt, your first pair of glasses (if applicable), that first awesome piece of jewelry you bought from the Renaissance fair. Fill this page with happy memories!

Found Your Voice Badge

"You've always had the power my dear, you just had to learn it for yourself."

It takes time to figure out what you want to say and how you want to say it. Being a geek gives you a certain set of tools and resources that can be very helpful: the power of your favorite story, the influence of your favorite character, the inspiration from all the amazing ideas you devour every day. It's from this mental database of varying viewpoints and concepts that you can start to build your own version of the world, and how you are going to tell everyone about it.

Geeky Source Material

Use the spaces to chart your inspirations and influences.

Source (movie, television show, book, etc.)	Most Important Lesson Taught

Hit Record and Save

What is the one thing you want everyone else to know—that one idea that has taken shape, the pearl in the irritated oyster of your brain, the wisdom that you have sifted and gleaned from your travels in the geek world? Now is the time to write it down, save it from drifting away like so many other thoughts do. Then you can come back later and decide what to do with it.

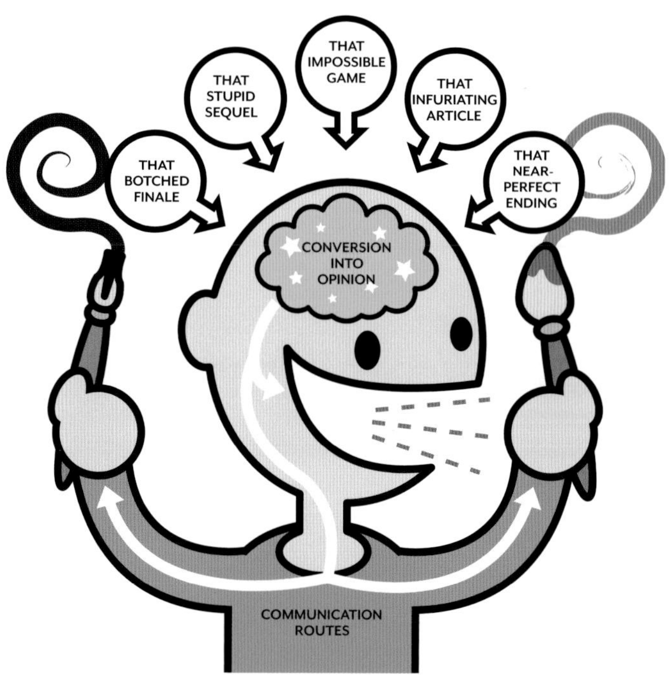

Feeding the Machine

Continual, insidious (and frankly just tiring) negative junk can actually be powerful in helping you find your voice. You can always choose to convert that destructive energy into creation instead.

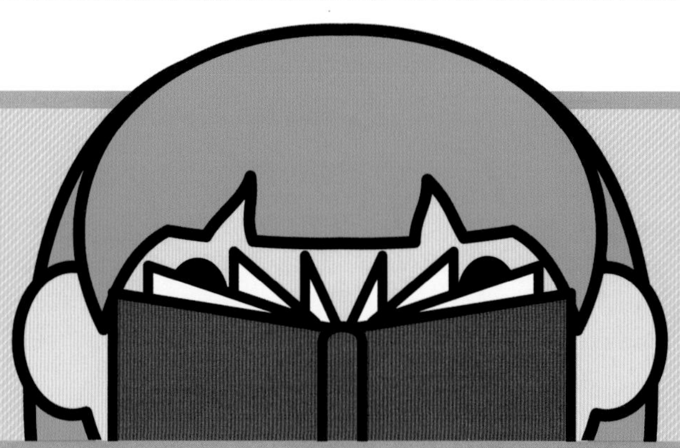

ABSORPTION MERIT BADGES

You have to feed the beast. Passion is always hungry, always greedy, always wanting more. You want to know everything about what you love—the how, the what, the why-in-the-hell. Your eyes and ears are just tubes that bring the good stuff to your ravenous mind. And that bastard never seems to be satisfied.

This section is all about how you challenge yourself, entertain yourself, and sometimes even learn in spite of yourself. You keep your doors open and your mind ready. Bring on the info dump!

Caffeine Command Badge

"Damn good coffee! And hot!"

With geeky passion comes the concurrent need for energy to fuel it. All that dedication and devotion (and occasional cheeky antics) requires high stamina, and yet sometimes you've got nothing left in your tank. This is the time for the careful and well-considered application of temporary stimulation: in other words, our good friend coffee and all its assorted colleagues and associates. There are things to do that are just waiting for you to do them! Screw you, entropy!

Tested and Approved Energy Sources

Use the checklist to keep track of your personal preferences in consumable vitality.

- ❑ tea
- ❑ coffee
- ❑ more coffee
- ❑ too much coffee
- ❑ energy drink
- ❑ energy drinks whose cans have the same color scheme as an industrial solvent
- ❑ dark forces
- ❑ natural giddiness

Artificial Energy Limitations

Once that limit is hit, it's all downhill. *Wheeeee!*

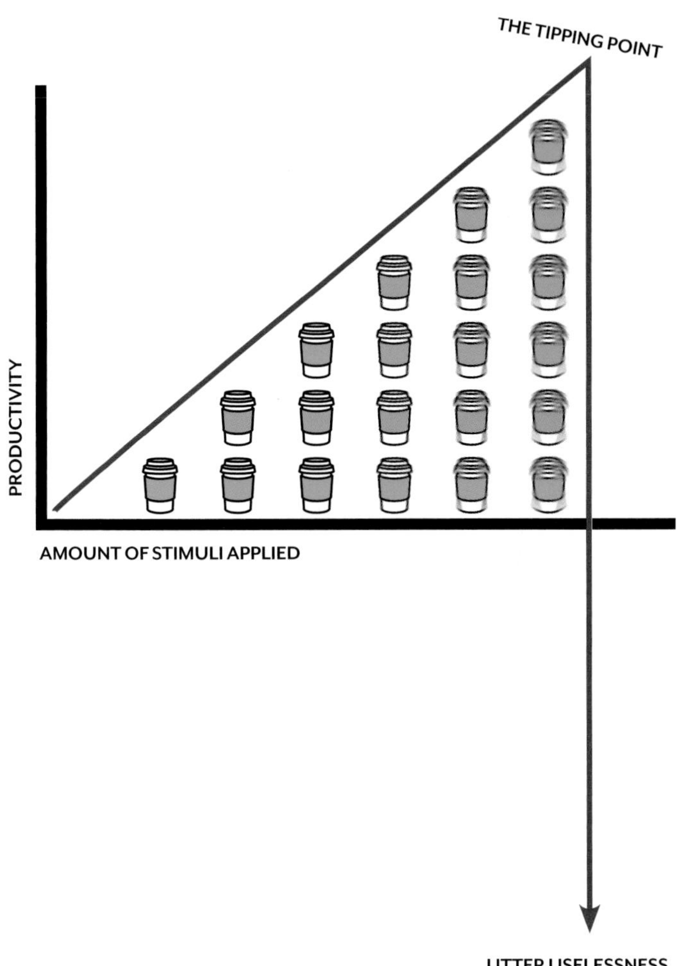

Identifying Energy Sucks

One way to help manage energy is to track where it all goes, and then stop any unintentional power leaks.

List ten activities or events that seem to particularly drain your geek enthusiasm levels, then rank them from one (most energy consuming) to ten (least energy consuming). Now you know who the biggest offenders are, and can decide what to do about them. Save your energy stores!

1. ....
2. ....
3. ....
4. ....
5. ....
6. ....
7. ....
8. ....
9. ....
10. ....

Plot Pathfinder Badge

"Trust me. I'm the Doctor."

Stories can be tricky beasts, sometimes roaming from one medium to another, crossing streams and changing lanes. But you, intrepid tracker, never lose sight and follow wherever that narrative goes. There may be bumps and bruises on the way, or switchbacks and course reversals, but a good geek doesn't give up easy. Love means never having to say reboot.

Quest Journal

Check off each medium through which you have undauntingly followed a single franchise, story or character.

The Dos and Don'ts of Successful Narrative Navigation

Moving from one medium to another can be a worrisome time for a loyal geek. You want to follow your favorite stories wherever they go, but changes will and must happen from adaptation to adaptation. This does not have to be a stressful process, especially if you keep these helpful dos and don'ts in mind.

Do:

- Take a deep breath.
- Accept this version for what it is.
- Remember that nothing is perfect.
- Seize the chance of an adventure.
- Bring an open mind, an open heart (and mostly likely an open wallet).

Don't:

- Read the comments sections.
- Pre-rage.
- Let nostalgia hold you hostage.
- Waste your energy on something you can't change.
- Worry. The original version you love still exists. A hundred adaptations and retellings and reinventions can never change that.

Is This Trip Necessary?

Need a quick and (almost) scientific way to figure out whether you want to take the leap into another medium with your favorite story?

First decide what the heart of the story is for you: that main core of goodness that makes it special. Is it a certain character or characters' relationship? Is it the world itself and its complicated mythos? Is it its heart-wrenching drama or its sharp wit?

Then use the chart to track your requirements, and figure out the true necessity of any multiplatform travel plans.

STORY	WHAT'S ITS HEART?	DOES THE NEW VERSION HAVE HEART?

Top Ten Badge

"You're the best around. / Nothing's ever gonna keep you down."

A place for everything, and everything in its place. Ranking, stacking, organizing—they're a way to deal with all the pop culture data that a passionate geek collects in the brain bin. We are often natural curators—not just wanting to acquire knowledge, but to process it and make it useful. Of course, there's an inherent danger in the weighing and measuring of subjective matters. Lists can create meaning—but they can end friendships too. Choose wisely.

Top Ten Ways Top Ten Lists are the Best

1. They are easy.
2. They are informative.
3. They are revealing.
4. They are efficient.
5. They are archival.
6. They are intuitive.
7. They are inspirational.
8. They are fun.
9. They are instant.
10. They are short.

Top Ten Ways Top Ten Lists are the Worst

1. They are shallow.
2. They are simplistic.
3. They are antagonistic.
4. They are manipulative.
5. They are limited.
6. They are reductive.
7. They are cheap.
8. They are lazy.
9. They are repetitive.
10. They are everywhere.

Top Ten Reasons for Top Ten Lists

1. Show off your impeccable taste.
2. Educate about awesomeness.
3. Advocate for the undeservingly unknown.
4. Explain the baffling.
5. Simplify the numerous and complicated.
6. Organize your ever-expanding knowledge base.
7. Remember the best bits.
8. Inspire new experiences.
9. Capture a certain time and place.
10. Share the too-good-to-keep-to-yourself stuff.

Top Six Reasons It's Usually a Top Ten List

1. There is historical precedent.
2. It has a sense of balance.
3. They're not so short as to be inconsequential.
4. And not so long as to be useless.
5. It's a nice round number.
6. Ending here just feels wrong.

Overlooked Rankings

Don't overlook the smaller, more uniquely personal categories for the top ten treatment. Rank all your stuff! Here are some examples to get you started.

Top Ten Best Movie Snacks:

....

....

....

....

....

Top Ten Songs That Get Stuck in My Head

....

....

....

....

....

Top Ten Shiny Things

....

....

....

....

....

Top Ten Personal Victories

Top Ten Procrastination Techniques

Constant Collector Badge

"Gotta catch 'em all!"

Geeks love the thrill of the chase, the satisfaction of completion. We came, we saw, we got the action figure. As geeks, we just don't want to visit our infatuations, we want to understand them, to hold a piece of them in our hands. Then maybe have a whole shelf of them. Or a whole room. Or a personal museum.

Collectible Desirability and Value Perception Chart

A far-too-common truth: The winds of fandom can be so fickle!

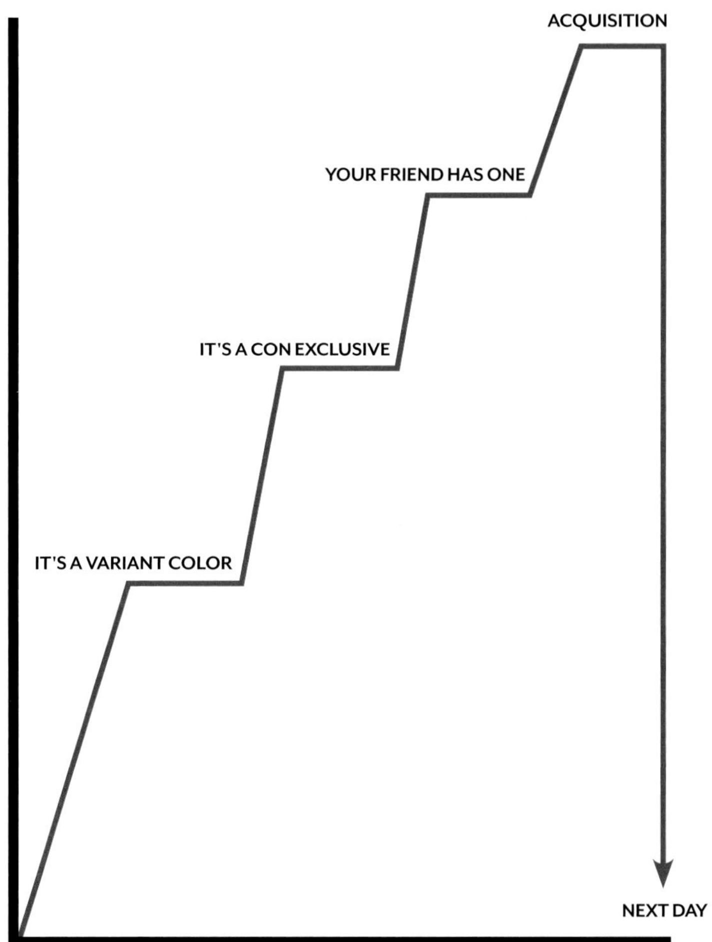

So Many Possible Collectibles

Want to start a collection but don't know where to start? Already have one but are thinking of diversifying? Do you collect collections and are you on the lookout for your next addition? Here are some suggestions for easy-to-get and relatively inexpensive items that might work for you.

buttons **mugs** **hats**

stickers **blind box toys***

A History of My Collection

There is a story behind every collection, and now is the time to record yours. Use the questions to start your own "Epic Tale of Things That I Love and Might Have Too Many of But I Don't Care Because They Are Amazing and I Can Always Buy Another Shelf!"

***This might drive you mad.**

What do you collect?

....

What is it about this particular thing that speaks to you?

....

What is your proudest acquisition?

....

What is your most embarrassing purchase?

....

What is one rare/discontinued/too expensive item that still eludes you?

....

What is the craziest thing you've done to add a piece to your collection? (Beware: This might constitute a written confession.)

....

Outrageous Rage Badge

"That's my secret, Captain: I'm always angry."

Unfortunately, geek passion has a dark side. If you give a crap about something, those strong emotions can easily slide right past love into anger before you know it. Although some good-old-fashioned righteous indignation can make you feel powerful at first, eventually it wears you down and leaves you sad, tired and in the exact same situation you were in before. Don't fall into that trap. You've got better uses for your talents.

The Art of Outsized Anger Maintenance

You can feel that dark storm gathering: your vision goes red and you feel a deep need to visit a comment thread and blast away with both barrels. Before you say or type something you might regret later, try using the following techniques instead.

Take a deep breath.

Count to ten.

Talk it out.

Dance it out.

Realize we are all but pebbles in the ever-flowing river of life.

Turn your computer off. (Maybe put a blanket over it to be safe.)

The Geek Serenity Meditation

If you ever feel like your head is going to explode in frustration over a reboot, a botched finale or a ridiculous piece of casting, try repeating this mantra a few times and see how you feel.

> Grant me the serenity to ignore the stuff I do not like,
> The courage to support the stuff I love,
> And the wisdom to remember the difference.

Geek Serenity in Action

Use the spaces to write down things that enrage you that you cannot change (at least at this point in time). Name them, acknowledge them, then let them go. They have no power over you.

Things I can't change:

- That director I hate keeps getting work.
- That writer I like is never going to finish his or her epic series.
- They rebooted that entire comic universe—again.

....

....

....

My Personal Rage Gauge

Before you can deal with anger, it helps to measure your levels to see if you are just a little hot under the collar or at a full tilt boil.

Fill in the chart to categorize what makes you upset at each level.

LEVEL ONE—MILDLY PERTURBED

LEVEL TWO—SOMEWHAT UPSET

LEVEL THREE—PRETTY PISSED

LEVEL FOUR—INCREDIBLY UPSET

LEVEL FIVE—BURN IT ALL!

Game Master Badge

"Greetings, programs!"

GAMES: They keep your brain limber, your heart pumping, and your killer instincts honed to a sharp edge. Whether with cards or boards or just pen and paper, games spontaneously break out wherever and whenever geeks gather. Maybe it's the puzzle-solving element or the fact that socializing with a clear purpose is often preferable to unfocused hanging out. In any case, geeks live for a good challenge.

Reasons to Love Board Games

perfectly detailed tokens

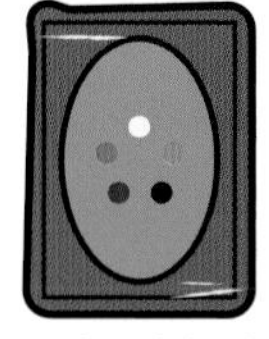
cards with battle damage

satisfaction of popping pieces out of a punchboard

the click of wood/plastic against the board

the purring zzzzt of a spin wheel

seeing the blood drain from your opponent's face as you move in for the kill

How to Recognize the Game Master Inside

Like games? Love games? *Love* games? Use the checklist to help find how much game is in you.

- ❑ Do you attend a regular game night?
- ❑ Do you host it?
- ❑ Do you own more than five board games?
- ❑ Own more than ten board games?
- ❑ Do you have a game closet?
- ❑ Do you have a game room?
- ❑ Do you have game house with space to sleep (if you move enough game boxes)?

- ❑ Have you had to ask "How many sides?" when someone requested dice?
- ❑ Have you ever checked a door for a trap in real life?
- ❑ Have you ever spontaneously smiled at the sight of a blank sheet of graph paper?
- ❑ Do you carry a deck of cards with you at all times?
- ❑ Have you ever created your own game?
- ❑ Have you ever talked others into playing your original game?
- ❑ Do you still talk to those people?

Known Friendship Enders: Is Winning Worth It?

Of course winning is worth it, but you should at least pretend to think about it first. Fill in the list of known pieces, moves and strategies that could possibly, probably or most definitely destroy a social circle or two.

Examples:

- Use Kneepads of Allure. (Munchkin)
- Block someone's longest road. (Settlers of Catan)
- Be not sorry. (Sorry)
- Do anything in Monopoly after the one hour mark. (Monopoly)

Your List of Doom

....

....

....

....

....

....

....

....

....

....

....

Eternal Student Badge

"You're gonna need a bigger boat."

There is just *so much stuff to know*! There is nothing more alluring than a puzzle to solve or a mystery to explore when you've got your geek burning strong. It's why we are usually never more than an arm's length from a book—or ten. It's why we take things apart, and time and interest permitting, put them back together. It's why our eyes are always open and our minds always seeking out those things we don't know... yet.

Common Objects of Adoration

Do you find yourself getting a little shiver of excitement or breaking out into a silly grin when you encounter any of the following?

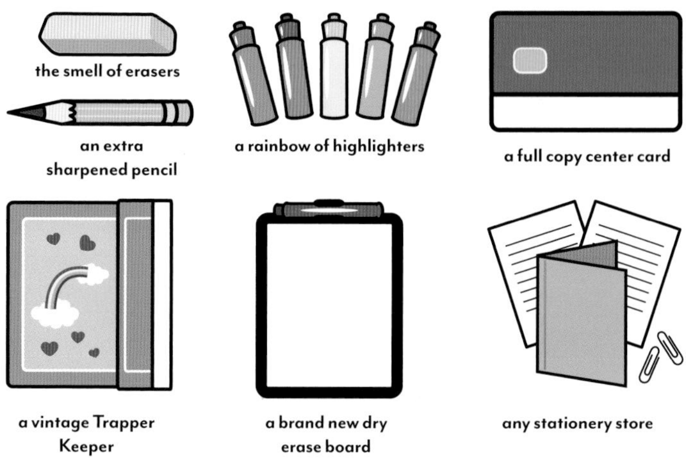

Common Signs You Never Stop Learning

Is your brain always hungry? Use the checklist to learn the sneaky feeding habits of your gray matter.

Do you:

- ❏ read books not for school?
- ❏ watch documentaries for fun?
- ❏ peruse a textbook for a subject you are not officially studying?
- ❏ consider a technical manual a casual read?
- ❏ drool in office supply stores?

❑ need more bookcases all the time?
❑ devour puzzles, crosswords and logic games?
❑ consider trivia night a full contact sport?.

How to Deal with Your Unread Books

It's a hazard of the geek lifestyle—too many books, not enough time. Use this how-to illustration to take care of the problem. (Sort of.)

1. Carefully gather your unread books.
2. Gently start stacking them.
3. Gingerly cut hole in your roof.
4. Casually allow your unread book stack to grow as tall as it needs to. You'll get to them. Eventually.

Speak the Language Badge

Geeks love language. Whether it's in the form of knowledge, nonsense or even the dreaded pun, words and what they do are forever fascinating. We enjoy words so much that we don't stop at real world vocabulary: We delve deep into fictional parlance as well. Can you grok that?

Check Your Fictional Language Expertise

Sometimes so-called real languages just aren't enough. Use the following checklist to see how much room fake lingo takes up in your real brain.

- ❏ Do you know a few words in a fictional language?
- ❏ Do you know a few phrases in a fictional language?
- ❏ Are you casually conversant in a fictional language?
- ❏ Have you written anything in a fictional language?
- ❏ Can you perform Shakespeare in a fictional language?
- ❏ Have you said wedding/commitment vows at least partly in a fictional language?
- ❏ Have you created your own fictional language?

A Grawlix of Fantastic Swears

Geeks have the most fantastic and colorful curse words. And the best thing is, you can use them and nobody will know how bad you just insulted them. That's playing smart.

frak ("Frak you!") **frell ("Frell you!")** **shazbot ("Oh shazbot!")**

Gorram ("Those gorram, Reavers!") **Smeg ("You're a total smeghead.")** **Poozer ("That Guy Gardner's a real poozer.")**

Get to Know Your Fictional Languages

Not every language is perfect for every occasion. Use the spaces to categorize the right languages for the right situations.

The one I'd use to sing a romantic ballad:

....

The one I'd use to insult my worst enemy:

....

The one I'd use to sound smart:

....

The one I'd use to lead an army:

....

The one I'd use to backstab my friends:

....

The one I'd use to rule the world:

....

Officially Obsessed Badge

"I've got a bad feeling about this."

There is a time when *love* doesn't quite describe your feelings anymore. It can seem such a pale and flimsy word to express your deep, all-encompassing passion. It's the first thing you're thinking of when you wake up, and the last thing to flit across your brain before you sleep. You want to write it, draw it, dress up as it—consume every last piece until you are more *it* than *you*. That is when you are officially obsessed. You are down the rabbit hole, and you are not sure if you want to come back. You've got it bad, and that can be good.

Percentage of Brain Activity Devoted to Obsession

A semiscientific study.

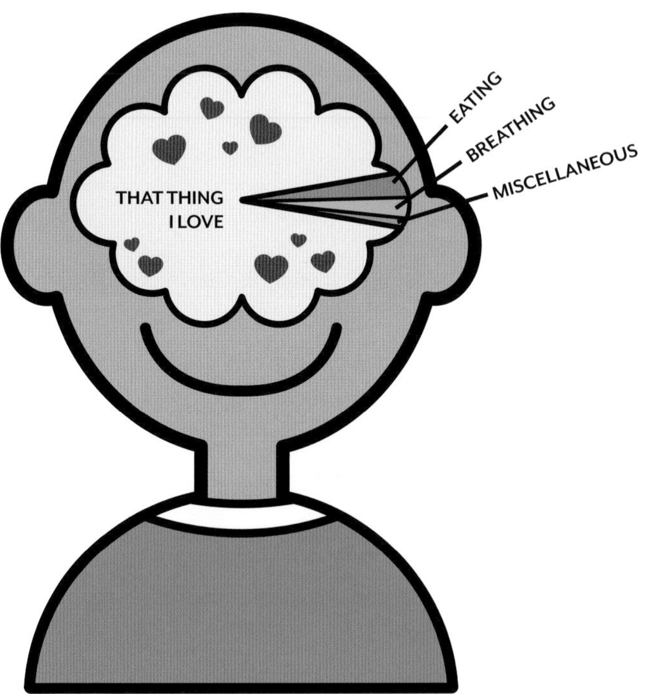

The Care and Feeding of an Obsession

Obsessions are ravenous beasts, always demanding more, more, more! To make sure its diet is varied and optimized, try a few selections from the menu.

- specialized books
- merchandise

- conventions
- fan fiction or doujinshi
- fan art
- forums
- podcasts/online shows
- documentaries, including making-ofs
- down the wiki hole

The Obsession Cycle

What has happened before will happen again. But that's okay; every obsession cycle leaves you with new knowledge and new ways of looking at the world. You don't have to love something at the same level all the time for it to be meaningful to you.

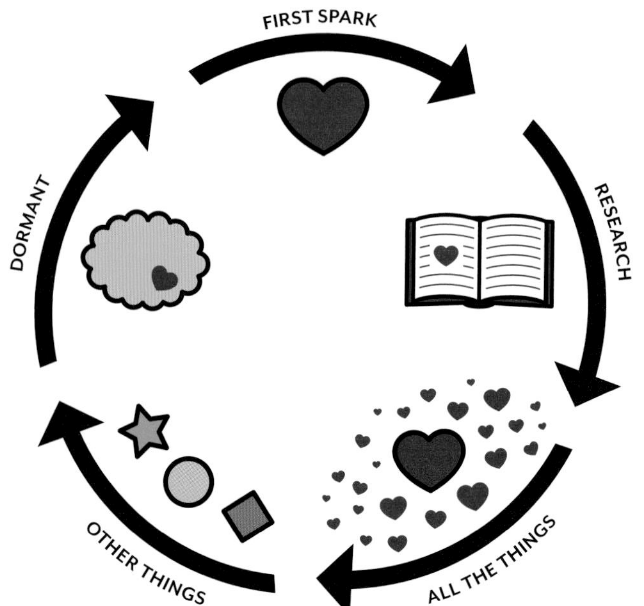

What are your obsessions and their first sparks?

Obsession: ....

....

First spark: ....

....

Obsession: ....

....

First spark: ....

....

Obsession: ....

....

First spark: ....

....

Obsession: ....

....

First spark: ....

....

Receiving on All Frequencies Badge

"As you wish."

Listen to others. Get out of your home genre. Vacation in another realm. There is so much that is unknown out there waiting to be discovered, but you have to be open and ready to hear its call. Geeks are at our best when plunging headfirst into the new, the wonderful, and the strange. So go forth, adventurer! Take notice of what others have to show you, and enjoy expanding your mind.

How to Stay Tuned In to a Coversation

- Ask questions.
- Don't get caught a nod loop.
- Pretend there will be a quiz afterward, and you want that A+.
- Pretend the speaker is your king or queen and you are his or her knight.
- Pretend the speaker is on your favorite podcast.
- Pretend you are a better listener than you are.

Recognizing Your Own Interface

To learn in the most receptive and efficient way possible, it helps to figure out how you gather and process information.

The Eye

- seeing
- drawing
- showing

You learn best with diagrams, pictures and infographics (your bestest friends).

The Ear

- hearing
- talking
- listening

You learn best with lectures, discussions and musical theater (if available).

The Hand

- physical
- touching
- acting

You learn best with activities, experiments and interpretative dance (be the information).

The Brain

- reading
- writing
- reflecting

You learn best with notes, lists and books (books 'n' books 'n' books).

Open Your Hailing Channels

Write a list of five things you're curious about in your geek life but haven't explored yet.

(Example: Understanding that popular book series, trying out cosplay, or starting a D&D campaign.)

1. ....
2. ....
3. ....
4. ....
5. ....

Pick the one you are most curious about right now.

....

Now write down three specific actions you can do to give it a try, and check off each action as you complete it.

(Ex. If I want to understand that popular book series, I can: 1) Pick up the first book and read a couple of chapters; 2) Go to a fan forum dedicated to the book series and read a thread or two without judgement; and 3) Ask someone I know who likes the series what it is about the books that speaks to him or her.)

1. ....
....

2. ....
....

3. ....
....

Rinse and repeat with the rest of your list. Feel your mind grow.

TRANSMISSION MERIT BADGES

You've always known that a shared geekery is a strong geekery. If something amazing happens and you can't tell your friends about it, is it still as amazing? Does it immediately get downgraded to frustrating instead? It's good geek manners to support what you love by telling everybody about why it kicks ass with the heat of a thousand feet.

This section is for strengthening your communications network on both the communal and the personal level. Learn how to shout it from the rooftops, sing it in the streets or wear it on your chest. Surround yourself with your geek.

Nostalgia Navigation Badge

"Valar Morghulis."

Visiting the past is tricky. As geeks, we revere the sights and sounds that shaped us into the people that we are today. But we can often fall victim to stultifying hero-worship and pedestal-placing as well. You can't freeze the past and sell it for a sentimental bounty, but you don't have to forget everything either. Find the middle ground.

Facing the Past

One way to clear out a little room in your nostalgia centers is to actually go back and re-experience the shows, movies and books you most idolize from your childhood and find out if they still hold up.

WARNING: Make sure you really want to do this. Decide if you'd rather keep the warm fuzzy memories, or risk the possibility that the younger you didn't have the best taste. Let's face it: Little you might have been kinda dumb.

SHOW/MOVIE/ BOOK I LOVED	DATE REVISITED	STILL LOVE IT?	ANY REGRETS?

Nostalgia Overload Warning Signs

Not sure if you are just wistfully remembering the good times or have gotten stuck in the past? Use the following checklist to see if you might be unknowingly caught in the open pit of unchecked nostalgia.

- ❑ You use the phrase "kids today."
- ❑ You can't name a new book, movie, comic or game that you've tried in the last year.
- ❑ You are legitimately angry that another actor is daring to play an established character.
- ❑ You take any criticism of a beloved childhood memory like it was a slap to your face.
- ❑ You hold grudges against people you've never met making work you'll never see because of misplaced anger of which you'll never let go.

Nostalgia Hacks

You might not be able to time travel (yet), but you can recreate certain childhood joys with some simple substitutions and a little creativity. Work out some ideas on the chart.

WHAT DO YOU MISS? ....

WHY? ....

CURRENT SUBSTITUTE? ....

EXAMPLE:

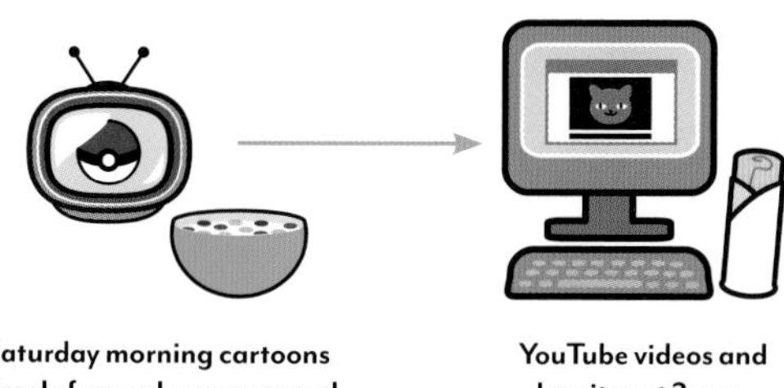

Saturday morning cartoons Simple fun and sugary cereal

YouTube videos and burritos at 2 a.m.

Extroverted Inversion Badge

"Wait till they get a load of me!"

Though many geeks are introverts, or at least have some introverted tendencies, that doesn't mean we don't want to be social. Quite the contrary: Geeks absolutely thrive in sharing knowledge, interests, and all sorts of cool stuff with others. Geeks are way more social than we are given credit for: We just tend to connect with others in different ways that aren't always recognized. People can be cool—at least in small amounts.

Geeking Out with Others

Use the checklist to tally how many geek-flavored social interactions you enjoy in a year. And yes, these all absolutely count: You might be social butterfly (or at least a convivial Mothra) even if you didn't know it.

- ❏ At a game/comic store
- ❏ At an arcade
- ❏ At a game night
- ❏ At a trivia night
- ❏ At a convention
- ❏ At a movie night
- ❏ On a video/text chat
- ❏ On a multiplayer game
- ❏ On a remote-yet-synchronized televion show or movie viewing

Pushing Your Boundaries

If you want to expand a bit beyond your regular socialization style, try on your extrovert suit and take it for a little stroll. Here are a few ideas to test out.

- Say "yes" to the next party invite you get. You can always leave whenever you want.
- Dye your hair a bright color. It breaks the ice for you.
- Let your picture get taken. Allow yourself to be seen at least once.
- Eat out by yourself. Be social by osmosis.
- Volunteer at something fun like a festival. Then you have to participate. Take that, shyness!

- Go on an adventure with an extroverted friend. Travel with your own personal social Sherpa.

Charging Station

After all the socializing and connecting and human interaction, don't forget to re-energize yourself when needed. Here are some suggestions to keep your power at optimum levels.

Persona Production Badge

"We are what we pretend to be, so we must be careful about what we pretend to be."

How do you present yourself to the world? And why? Geeks know all about alter egos and secret identities, and we are often very willing to try different versions of ourselves to see what sticks. Trying to build the best you is one of the best puzzles there is, and sometimes just one you is not enough—you are legion.

The Benefits of a Virtual Avatar

- It gives you freedom to explore different facets of your personality.
- It's a chance to try various ways to express your thoughts.
- You have the ability to expand your social boundaries slowly and safely.
- You can increase connectivity with other inspiring personalities.
- You can discover (and hopefully divest yourself of) any hidden jackass tendencies.

Offline Avatar Maker

Need a visual version of your persona for social media, but can't find the right online avatar creator? Go lo-fi. Color the pieces, then cut and paste your way to individuality!

Believe It or Not, It's Just Me

To become the person you want to be, you first must figure out just what the hell that actually means to you. What are the elements of that super amazing and fantastic geek that you know you can be?

What kind of geek do I want to be?
(**EXAMPLE:** I want to be brave.)

- I want to be ....
- I want to be ....
- I want to be ....
- I want to be ....
- I want to be ....
- I want to be ....
- I want to be ....

Write down one doable action for each quality, then check it off when you do it.
(**EXAMPLE:** To be a brave geek, I will ride that roller coaster that scares the hell out of me.)

- To become ...., I will ....!
- To become ...., I will ....!
- To become ...., I will ....!
- To become ...., I will ....!
- To become ...., I will ....!
- To become ...., I will ....!
- To become ...., I will ....!

Awesomeness Ambassador Badge

"

"I've seen things you people wouldn't believe."

You are a champion for the things you love and you want to share them with the world. Geek enthusiasm is one of our greatest gifts, and we are not selfish with the good stuff. We are envoys for the best stories, promoters of brilliant creators, and the connection points between the waiting-to-be-found and those that search. Pass it on!

How to Recognize You've Found the Awesome

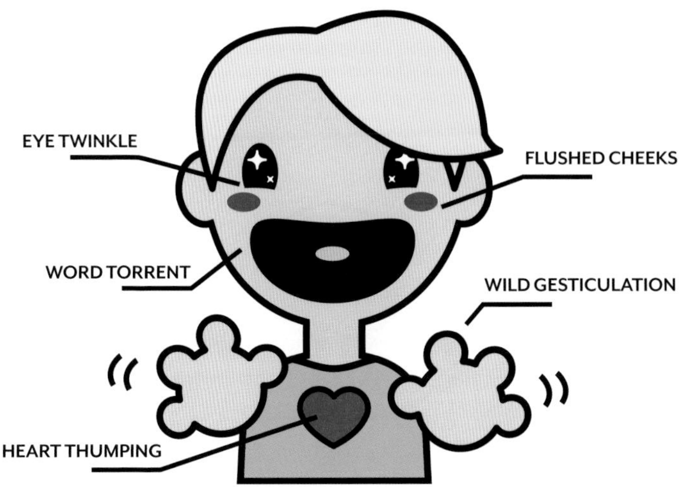

Warning Signs of Disengagement

Unfortunately, not everyone is ready to hear what you have to say. Here are a few signs to look for that might mean your audience is not as receptive to your geeky proselytizing as you had hoped.

- The only responses you've gotten in the last half hour are a mix of "hmm" and "ahhum."
- All of a sudden the floor tile pattern seems to become super interesting to them.
- You don't hear their phone ring, but they put it to their ear and start talking anyway.
- They've got lifeless eyes. Black eyes. Like a doll's eyes.

- They gnaw off their own shoulders and weep blood.

How an Awesome Infection Spreads

Once you share with someone your joy and enthusiasm, they pass it on to others, and then those others pass it on—and soon a rabid fandom is born. Transmit the awesome!

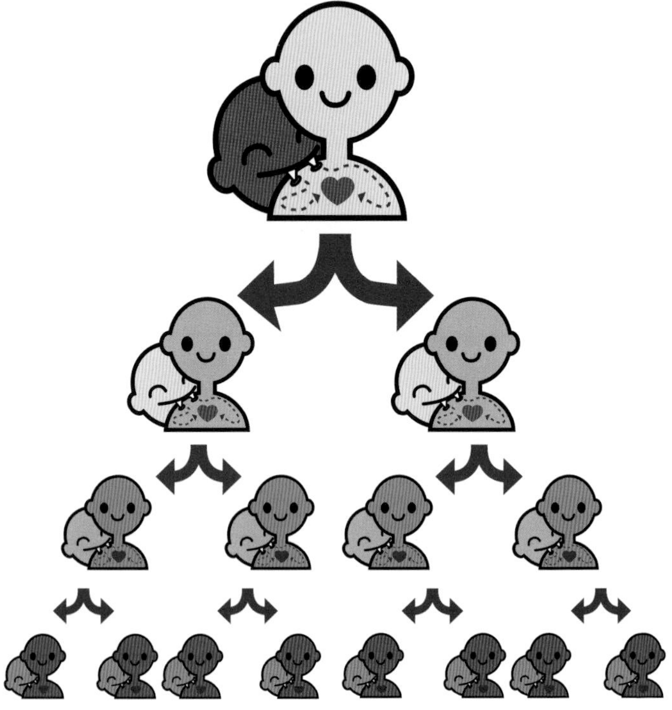

A Cold Call Script

Want to convince someone to try that fantastic show you just binge watched or that unbelievably great game you just finished over the weekend—but you have no idea where to start? Use the following template to craft a thoughtful and reasoned script.

> "Hi friend. You may know me from *[work / school / the neighborhood / just generally around]* (circle one). You strike me as a person with the requisite *[good taste / sense of humor / flair and élan / adequate brain functions]* (circle one) to appreciate *[name of thing you want them to try]*.
>
> Please don't be put off by my *[directness / intensity / one crazy eye / slight moistness]* (circle one), I just feel I couldn't live with myself if I didn't tell you about how *[name of thing you want them to try]* has all the *[a positive quality]* and the *[another positive quality]* you seem to be missing in your life.
>
> I am sure that if you just give *[that thing this whole spiel is about]* a try, you will feel *[good/complete/happy/almost sure I won't bother you again]* (circle one). Thank you for your time.

Welcoming Committee Badge

"Well, welcome home to Happiness Hotel..."

We were all new once. We all have the first time we saw that movie we now know by heart; or the first time we read that first chapter in the first book of our favorite series; or the first time we bought that first comic and placed it in our first longbox. A good geek is always ready to welcome another member into the fold. There is power in numbers.

Open the Doors Wide

The geek tribe is a large and hearty one. Exclusion is the antithesis of the true geek spirit of searching, studying and sharing. Keep the following points in mind to make sure our geek culture stays something of which we can all be proud and all be an equal part.

- There is no hierarchy of fandoms: books = manga = cosplay = RPGs = fan fiction.
- Nobody speaks for all geeks.
- Everyone has a right to their own style and amount of enthusiasm.
- There are no tests or quizzes to be a "real geek."
- Speak up and shut down jerks. They make us all look bad.
- Share what you love. It won't run out.

Foolproof Geek Detection Chart

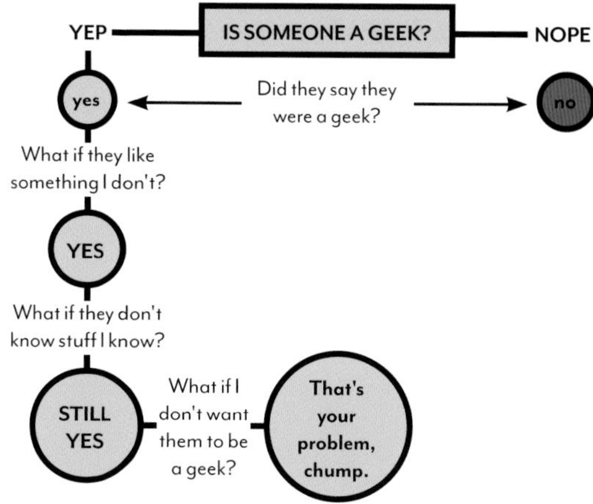

A Geek Starter Kit

If you could bestow any important gifts on someone who was just about to embark on a new life of geekery, what would they be and why? Add your own ideas to the suggestions.

- **FEARLESSNESS:** Always try new things and keep exploring the awesome.
- **INNER CALM:** Trust yourself and follow your passions.
- **OUTER CALM:** Deal with the assorted idiots, trolls and jackasses that lurk in every group and culture.
- **PLUCK:** Keep picking yourself up, dusting yourself off, and geeking all over again.
- **HUMOR:** You'll need it. Trust me.

....

....

....

....

....

Lending Library Badge

"It's a moral imperative."

At least half of your books and other physical media are in other people's hands right now, and that's the way you like it. Sharing is an important geeky tradition, and there is something magical about placing a new adventure into someone's open hand and knowing that the next time you meet, that person will be changed.

A Stark Truth

This diagram doesn't lie. Lending comes with risks, but introducing someone to their new favorite thing is always worth the risk.

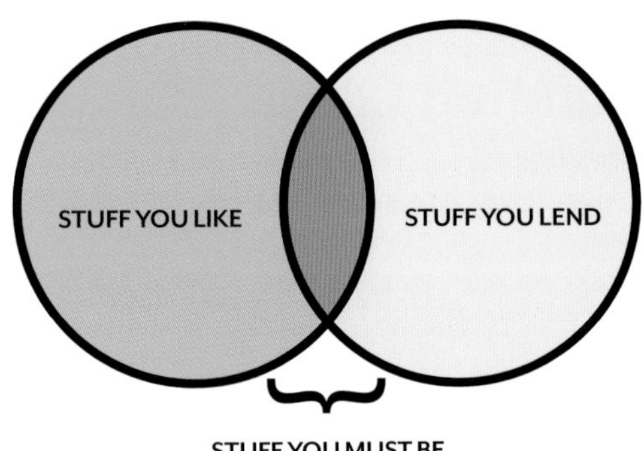

Why Lend Books?

What is it about sharing books that is so satisfying?

- It's like giving someone a mystery to solve.
- You feel like you are doing good work.
- You can get a book to borrow in return.
- Getting someone to try something new is easier in person. Go peer pressure!
- You can threaten to spoil the ending right to someone's face. **WARNING:** This is only for friends you want to rapidly convert into enemies.

Create Your Own Book Plates

When you are lending books out, it doesn't hurt to have a casual reminder that *eventually, at some point, it'd be cool if this returned home.* Photocopy this book plate, cut it out, and place it in the next novel you let someone share. It might actually work.

This Book Belongs To:

____

It is a good book, that is why you borrowed it in the first place.

Good books deserve to go home.

Don't make this book sad.

Poor, sad lonely book.

You are a monster.

Mighty Mentor Badge

"Do not meddle in the affairs of wizards."

We all started alone once. But usually there was someone—a parent, sibling, friend or even the work of a favorite author—that became our mentor and guided us into the wonderful world of geekiness. As a good geek, you should be ready, willing and able to return that favor someday to the next generation. You can be that sympathetic ear and guiding hand, sharing all your hard-won wisdom and passing on all the important stories. Everyone begins as the companion, but when you are ready, you can be the Doctor.

Classic Mentor Archetypes

There is more than one approach to being a teacher and guide. Take some inspiration from some of the different mentor types.

Spiritual

EXAMPLES: Yoda, Master Splinter, Morpheus

STYLE: patient, calm, sometimes frustratingly vague

Mischievous

EXAMPLES: Uncle Iroh, Ms. Frizzle, Willy Wonka

STYLE: jovial, loves riddles, often what seems to be nonsense turns out to be the lesson itself

Tough Love

EXAMPLES: Granny Weatherwax, Professor McGonagall, Batman

STYLE: no-nonsense, sink-or-swim, everything is a test

Classic Wizard

EXAMPLES: Gandalf, Merlin, Obi-Wan Kenobi

STYLE: wise, mysterious, obligatory beard

Spiritual

Mischievous

Tough Love

Classic Wizard

How to be a Mentor

- Be committed.
- Be open.
- Be patient.
- Be positive.
- Be ready to learn as much as you teach.
- Be aware that your protege may surpass you someday, and it will take all your control not to drown in a sea of resentment and jealousy.

Your Repository of Enlightenment

What is most vital for you to pass down to the ages? What life lessons have you learned that you absolutely need to impart? Use this worksheet to collect and preserve your precious words of wisdom for the next generation (before you forget them yourself).

- The three most important things in life are .... , ..., and ....
- Never trust a person who..
- Always carry a..
- Beware of smiling ....
- Never judge a book by its cover—unless it has a ....on it.
- Always remember to.. before you ....

Disaster Preparedness Badge

"Can't we just get beyond Thunderdome?"

Geek culture has always had one foot in the future—and sometimes that future isn't looking so good. Many different flavors of apocalypse are part of the geek canon, as well as an almost equal number of survival techniques. Most of us have thought about what we'd do when it all went pear-shaped, and if nothing else, that makes us appreciate what we have right now even more. And maybe it reminds us to treat our computers nicer. Just in case.

Are You Ready?

They are many different forms the end of the world might take, but as a good geek, you are well versed in a variety of active planetary destruction scenarios, such as the following.

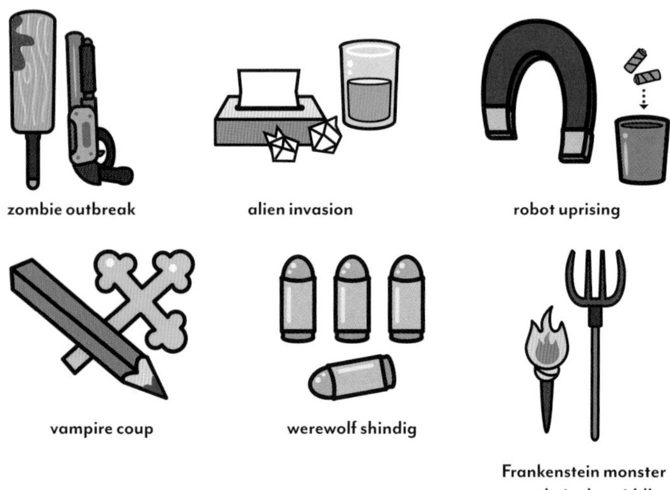

Being in the Now

Planning for all sorts of apocalypses also has the side effect of making you more grateful for your life as it is now. Try to enjoy the world while it isn't actively ending by using the following suggestions.

- Look up and enjoy the beautiful, blue, not-scorched sky.
- Appreciate the lack of feral child tribes looking to you for salvation.

- Celebrate the fact your food is (most likely) not people.
- Welcome being able to live past thirty without having to get "renewed."
- Love having your brains not on the menu.
- Be thankful machines don't want to kill you (probably).
- Be happy you are not a pod person (again, probably).

My Apocalyptic Dream Team

Do you know who'll have your back when it all hits the fan? Think about the people in your life that you'd want to face the end of the world with and why. Plan out your lineup with this worksheet.

NAME	SKILLS	POSITION IN THE GROUP

Advanced Armor Badge

"Your clothes. Give them to me. Now."

What you wear can be the perfect extension of your own geek self. Whether it's a T-shirt emblazoned with your favorite movie's logo, a pair of earrings shaped like retro gaming controllers, or a replica of a hat from your favorite show—they let the world know what you are passionate about. Plus, it can just make you feel good. Even if you aren't Superman, bearing that "S" on your chest can make you aspire to be as super as you can be that day.

T-Shirt Totality Chart

Geeks and T-shirts: a true love affair. They are the start, and sometimes the whole, of a geeky wardrobe. They are cheap, plentiful and cater to every fandom possible. The real problem comes with knowing when to stop.

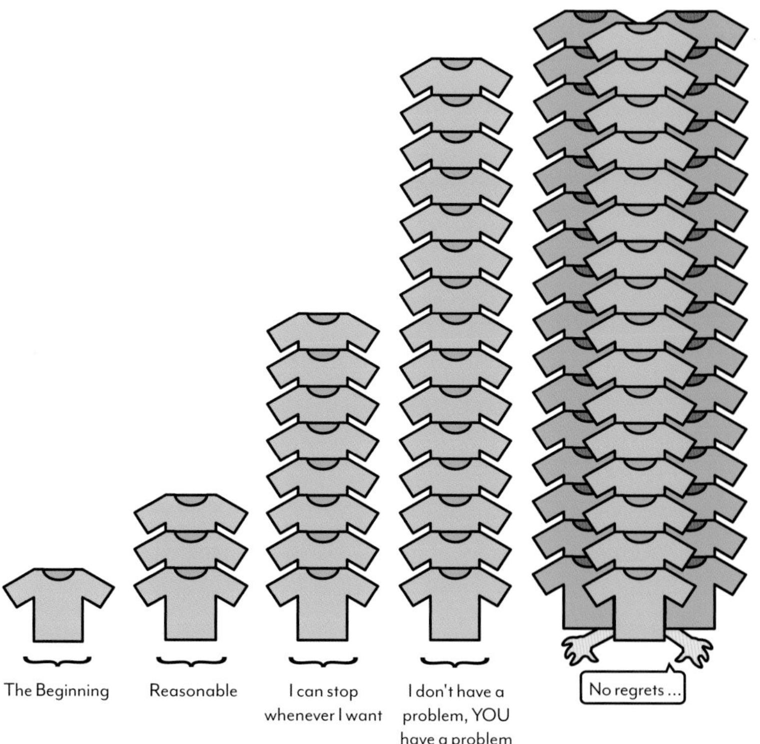

Hoodie: All-Purpose Awesomeness

What is it about the humble hoodie that explains its near ubiquitousness in the geek closet? Why does this simple modified jacket hold a special place in our hearts? Here are some of the hoodie's most positive attributes.

- **ALL-PURPOSE:** It's perfect for layering. You can go from indoor to outdoor geekery with ease.
- **USEFUL:** Hoodie strings can be employed as emergency fasteners or splint ties.
- **CAMOUFLAGE:** You can hide in your hood.
- **VERSATILE:** Wearing the hood up allows you to pretend to be anything from a casual monk, a wizard or even a Nazghul.
- **FUN:** Central location of the pocket makes you feel like a kangaroo.

My Power Suit

Wearing certain favorite pieces of clothing can change your whole mood and make you feel more ready to face whatever challenges the day has planned for you. Using the chart, equip yourself with your perfect power suit.

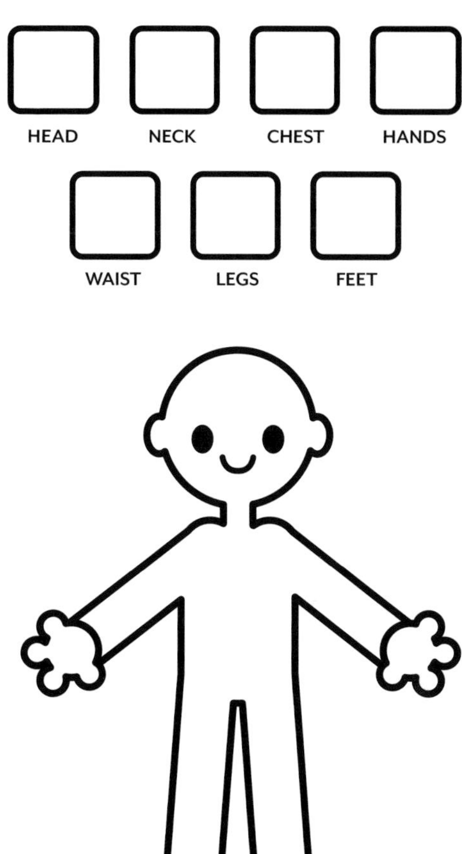

ACCESSORY SLOTS

Keeper of Traditions Badge

"Stay awhile and listen."

Don't forget the geeks that came before you: the fan club creators, the zine writers, the convention founders. And don't let the new geeks-in-training go forth without being proud of who they are and where they come from, either. Bang the drums, gather around the fire, and spread the tales of wonder and legends of old that keep the geek from burning out.

Classic Geek Traditions and the Lessons They Teach

Here are some of the oldest and most revered of geek customs, and reasons why it is important for them to continue for generations to come.

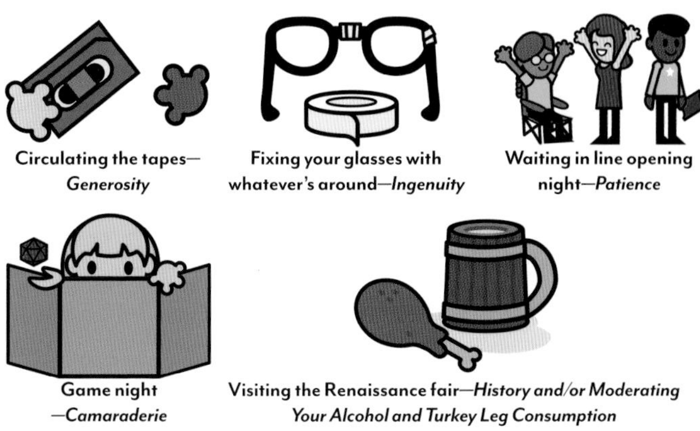

Circulating the tapes—*Generosity*

Fixing your glasses with whatever's around—*Ingenuity*

Waiting in line opening night—*Patience*

Game night—*Camaraderie*

Visiting the Renaissance fair—*History and/or Moderating Your Alcohol and Turkey Leg Consumption*

My Custom List of Customs

Write a list of your own personal geek traditions: those things you did when you were younger or still do now that help define your particular style of geekery.

EXAMPLES: Watching British sci-fi late Saturday nights on PBS. Curling up in a favorite chair with a fresh stack of comics.

1. ....
2. ....
3. ....
4. ....
5. ....

That New, Old-Time Tradition!

Inspired? Then use the following worksheet to plan out your very own personalized geek ritual you can share with some lucky friends, or just celebrate by yourself in solemn reflection. It's all up to you!

Name of your new tradition:

....

....

....

When it's observed:

....

....

....

Do you need any special items/equipment/accoutrements?

....

....

....

Describe how this tradition works:.

....

....

....

What does this tradition mean to you?

....

....

....

CREATION MERIT BADGES

Now it's time to give back. To make your own mark. To sing your own song. Consumption needs to be balanced with creation to keep the whole Wheel of Geek turning. Plus the world wants to see what you've got. Take all the fantastic stuff you've absorbed and process it through your own gears and cranks—and see what comes out the other side.

This section is for the maker in every geek. Whether it's through art or music, with scissors or violins, totally sensible or simply weird—there are more ways than you'll ever know to add your own piece to the universe. Play on!

Fan Fiction Finesse Badge

"Make it so."

The magic of fan fiction is interacting with the stories and characters you love while creating your own piece of that world. You can feed your imagination and spread your own literary wings by expanding the stories that speak to you the most. The story never has to end.

Your Fan Fiction Level

Need to test your fan fiction levels? Use the checklist to find out.

- ❑ Have you ever read fan fiction?
- ❑ Have you ever read fan fiction longer than the source that inspired it?
- ❑ Have you read *all* the fan fiction?
- ❑ Have you ever written your own fan fiction?
- ❑ Have you ever created a new character in your fan fiction?
- ❑ Have you ever published a slightly altered fan fiction that lead to a highly lucrative publishing contract? (You never know.)

The Health Benefits of Fan Fiction

Fan ficton helps keep your imagination happy and whole. It:

- flexes the writing muscles.
- employs practical creativity.
- teaches attention to detail.
- helps develop narrative consistency (or enough awareness to actively choose to eschew it).
- improves ability to deal with limitations creatively.
- alleviates the frustrations of waiting for official follow-ups.

The Perfect Mary Sue or Gary Stu Generator

It's okay. Why wouldn't you want to be the best part of an amazing, magical, adventure-filled world? Come on, indulge a little. Use these questions to create an embarassingly idealized self-insert character. Sue it up!

My name is ....

My eyes [are blue / are violet / change color with my emotions] **(CIRCLE ONE)**.

My ears are [pointy / not pointy / cat's ears] **(CIRCLE ONE)**.

I have [long / very long / magically long] **(CIRCLE ONE)** hair that never tangles and is a breathtaking shade of [shocking white / midnight black / deepest purple / palest pink] **(CIRCLE ONE)**.

I am [16 years old / 21 years old/ secretly thousands of years old/ extra secretly countless eons old] **(CIRCLE ONE)**.

I am special because [all the people I know are in love with me / I have a secret amazing power / I am the child of two of the established characters / I am the Chosen One who supersedes any established Chosen One in the canon / ....

....

....]

(CIRCLE AS MANY AS YOU LIKE; ADD MORE IF NEEDED).

In the end I [defeat the almighty evil / win the game / discover I am long-lost royalty / marry my favorite character / marry all my favorite characters and they are all cool with it / become the captain of the starship] **(CIRCLE ONE).**

Crafty Crafter Badge

"They've gone to plaid!"

The crafty possibilities are endless. With enough time, patience and force of will, almost any material can be stitched, glued, nailed or stretched into something truly amazing. And when you add the focused ingenuity and passion of a geek—that's when magic happens. Go and make stuff!

So Many Crafty Possibilities

Use this checklist to see how many crafts you've tried, and which ones you should try next.

The Art of Geekcraft

Why are crafts such a perfect way to demonstrate strong geekitude? Here are some reasons.

- Crafting can be both introspective *and* social.
- You get to play with sharp scissors and hot liquid glue.
- You can get as cute as you want.
- Getting three-dimensional adds depth to your fandom.
- You can show off your megatalents.

- Can't find merchandise for your favorite show? Make your own!
- It's hard not to feel like a badass when you can make a perfect weapon replica.

What Kind of Craft Is For Me?

Take this quick quiz to see what style of craft best suits your personality:

1. I prefer:
    a. putting things together.
    b. making things look nice.
    c. tearing things apart.

2. I make crafts because:
    a. I like the process.
    b. I like the purpose.
    c. I like the mess.

3. My favorite crafting tool is:
    a. a needle and thread.
    b. a hammer and tongs.
    c. scissors.

4. My dream crafting space is:
    a. a cozy sewing room.
    b. a well-equipped shed.
    c. wherever the glue gun is.

5. My crafting philosophy:
    a. "Every stitch counts."
    b. "My tools are an extension of myself."
    c. "Let's crack a beer and do this!"

Mostly As—Textile crafts (knitting, weaving, quilting)
Mostly Bs—Decorative crafts (metalworking, stained glass, furniture making)
Mostly Cs—Destructive crafts (creative chaos)

Command Center Badge

"To infinity... and beyond!"

Strive to make your ordinary everyday life just a little more extraordinary. Free your design geek to play, and make the space around you reflect the marvels inside. Why live in a boring rectangle filled with more boring rectangles, when you can create your own personal headquarters? Decorate with some geek flair!

Quick Ways to Geekify Your Room

Try some of these simple switches to add a unique (or just weird) touch to any humdrum room.

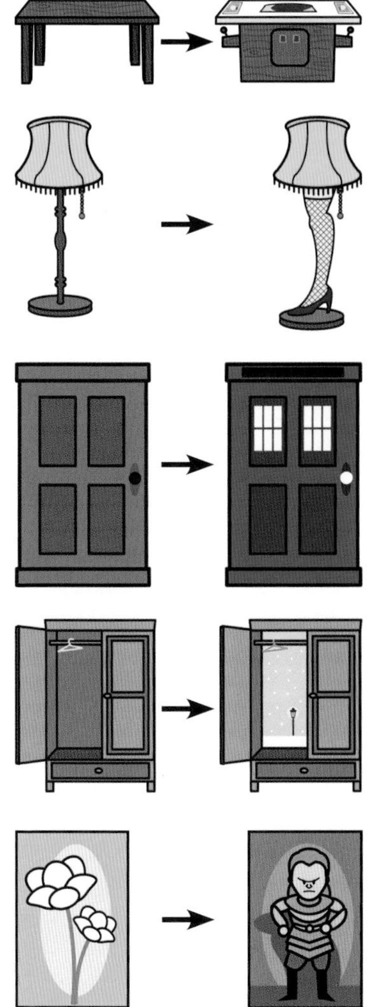

Home Is Where Your Laser Cannon Is

Need some inspiration? Check out this list of classic headquarters.

- The Batcave (Everyone needs their own Alfred.)
- The Fortress of Solitude (Bring a pair of mittens.)
- Sanctum Sanctorum (It just *sounds* cool, right?)
- The Gotham Clock Tower (Perfect for birds or bats.)
- 221B Baker Street (Comes with housekeeper.)
- Ghostbuster's Firehouse (Who doesn't love a fireman's pole?)
- 12 Grimmauld Place (Great defenses. Lousy service.)
- Captain's Ready Room (Simple. Classic.)

What Headquarters Style Fits You the Best?

1. Which main color would you prefer?
   a. polished steel
   b. warm brass
   c. nuclear pulsating green

2. What kind of lighting would you like?
   a. general ambient glow
   b. candles and braziers
   c. the only safety is in darkness

3. What's your preferred method of heating?
    a. silent computer-controlled vents
    b. crackling fireplace
    c. garbage can blaze

4. What room accent appeals to you most?
    a. a wall-sized monitor
    b. a worn wooden table
    c. a twisted chunk of metal

5. What is your most common emotion?
    a. optimistic wonder
    b. fantastical amazement
    c. "Run!"

Mostly A's—Futuristic spaceship bridge
Mostly B's—Magic workshop
Mostly C's—Post-apocalyptic dystopian hellhole

Inky Fingers Badge

"See You Space Cowboy..."

Geeks love fan art. From beautiful interpretations of favorite characters, to original work inspired by a book series, to quirky fun mashups—creativity and talent find an ideal pool of inspiration in fandom. When we were children, no matter what our innate artistic capabilities were, we drew superheroes or movie characters or fairy tale princesses. Fan art is that instinct grown up.

Are You a Fan of Fan Art?

Check off anything that sounds familar.

- ❑ I've browsed a fan art site.
- ❑ I've commissioned a fan art piece.
- ❑ I've drawn fan art.
- ❑ I've created an avatar of my favorite character to represent myself.
- ❑ I've created an inspirational quote poster.
- ❑ I've created an animated GIF from a favorite television show or movie.

Choose Your Instrument

So many ways to make a mark. What one fits you?

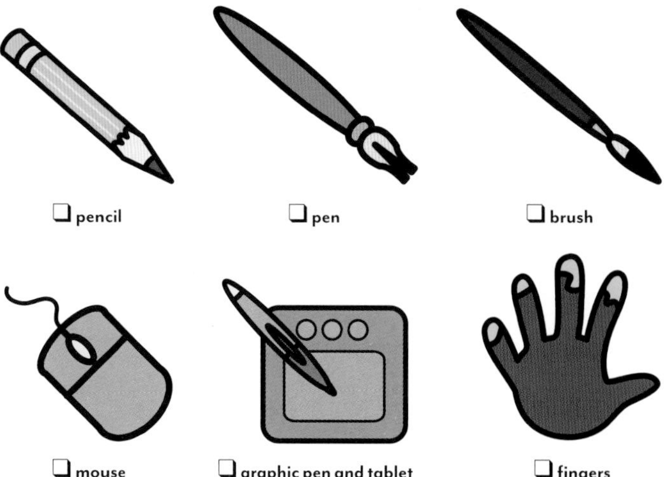

My First Fan Art

Add items listed next to each blank figure to make some quick fan art. You did it!

Katniss Everdeen

+ bow and arrow
+ long braid
+ a handful of nightlock berries (and nothing to lose)

Sherlock

+ deerstalker hat
+ pipe
+ sense of superiority

Spock

+ pointy ears
+ Starfleet uniform
+ sense of superiority

Link

+ pointy ears
+ pointy hat
+ pointy hair

Joker

+ green hair
+ red mouth
+ scars (but don't ask him where he got them)

Chewbacca

+ bandolier
+ fur
+ more fur

Tinker/Hacker/Fixer Badge

"Never give up. Never surrender."

You know everything can always be better, faster, stronger. Maybe even a little more awesome. Perfection might not exist, but geeks are almost positive there is a parking space right next to it. It's all part of the useful optimism that is one of the best parts of the whole geek package.

A Hacker Mind-Set

Here's a peek inside a mind always ready to make something better. A hacker believes:

- Anything that is broken can be fixed.
- Anything slow can be faster.
- Anything stuck can be unstuck.
- Anything wasteful can be more efficient.
- Anything in one piece can just as easily be in many.

A Tinkerer's Tool Kit

The more stuff lying around the house, the better. A full eighty percent of all life hacks involve one or more of the following items.

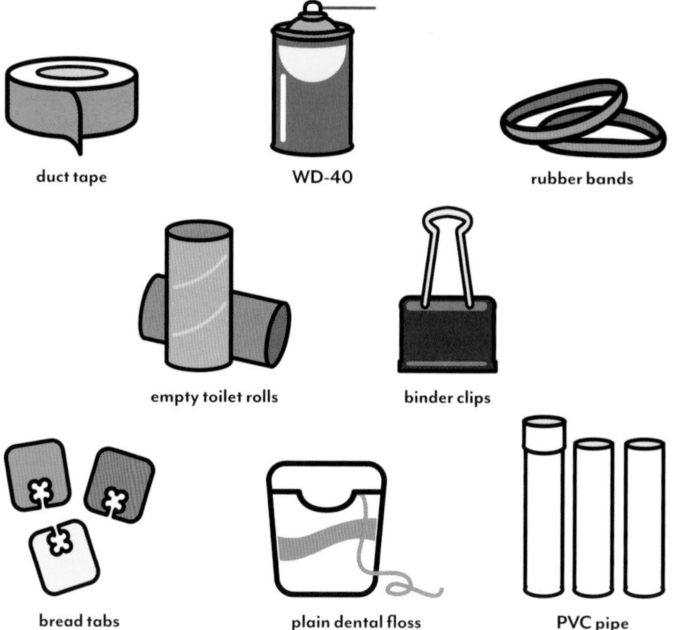

Just Because You Can Doesn't Mean You Should

It's easy to get caught in the excitement of fixing and hacking and experimenting. But now is the time to write a list of things it's probably best you don't mess with. Perhaps based on lessons already learned—or eyebrows already scorched.

EXAMPLE: Anything with a live current.

....

....

....

....

Cosplay Commando Badge

"Don't dream it. Be it."

You dream of being someone else sometimes—of wearing a hero's cloak, or a space captain's uniform, or an alien's skin. There is something deeply geeky in taking the leap and becoming another, allowing yourself the freedom to explore and interact with the world in a new and divergent way. It's part of the no-fear attitude a good geek develops to better enjoy all the universe has to offer. Change your outfit and change your world.

I'm Pulling the Wig Down From the Shelf

Here are just a few of the reasons why cosplaying is simply smashing. It:

- Shows devotion to a character
- Demonstrates your love of performance
- Develops community
- Encourages socializing
- Showcases your talent
- Grows self-confidence
- Is fun

Variations on a Theme

Spice up a costume. Interpret it. Put your own spin on it. Here are some suggestions.

Who Do You Want to Be?

What is your dream costume—the one you've always wanted to create and wear to blow everyone away with your genius? Even if you've never ventured into the realm of cosplay before, let yourself imagine the possibilites.

CHARACTER	HOW	WHY

Creative Cookery Badge

"The snozzberries taste like snozzberries."

What better way to experience fandom than through your stomach? So many stories feature tempting descriptions of treats and mouthwatering feasts. Sometimes when you are reading you can almost smell the grilling meat, baking bread and exotic desserts. Geeks want the full experience, and that absolutely includes taste. Embrace your geekery with relish!

Famous Fictional Foods

Along with their cheap common world counterpoints.

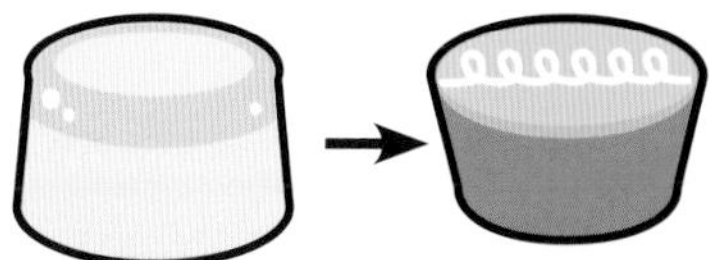

Lemon cakes (*Game of Thrones*)—**prepackaged orange cupcakes**

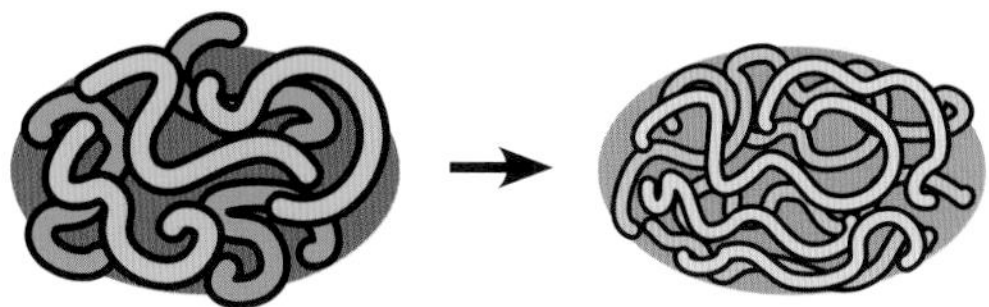

Klingon gagh (*Star Trek*)—**spaghetti**

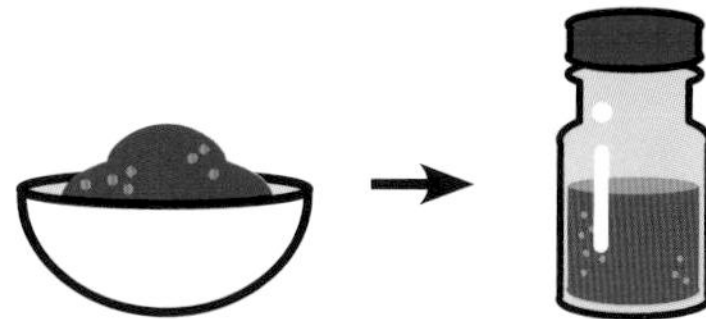

Melange (*Dune*)—**paprika**

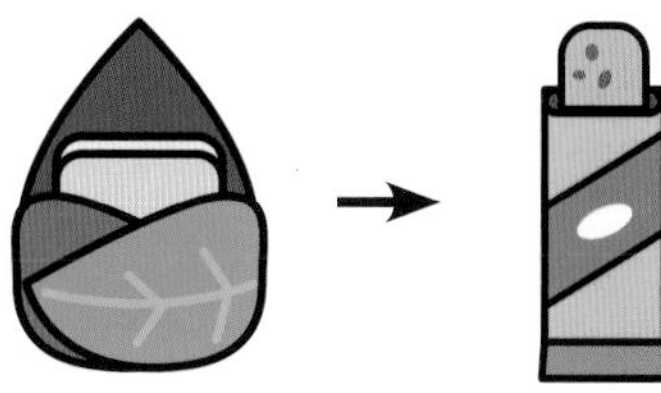

Lembas (*The Lord of the Rings*)—**energy bar**

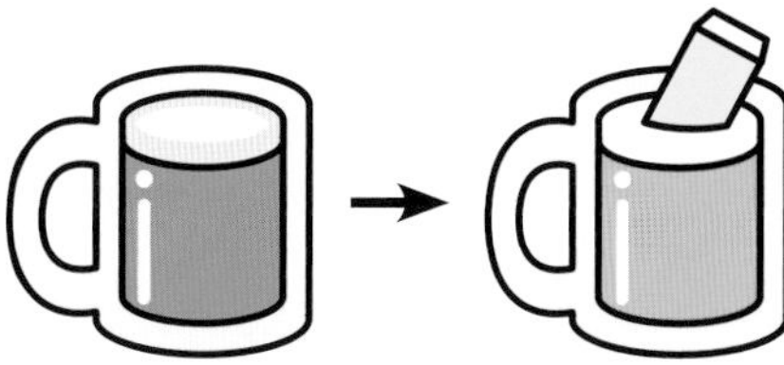

Butterbeer (*Harry Potter*)—**butter in beer**

Traditional Gaming Snacks

- Mountain Dew
- Cheetos
- Coke
- Doritos
- Chicken wings
- Beer
- Gummy worms
- Pizza (sometimes in roll form)

Don't Forget to Hydrate

Drinks we wish existed—and what they probably taste like.

- Slurm—syrupy addiction
- Moloko Plus—milk with a hint of opiates and violence
- Bantha milk—blue dye #1
- Slusho!—a Slurpee of an undisclosed flavor
- Raktajino—industrial strength espresso
- Romulan ale—a slap to the face
- Pan Galactic Gargleblaster—infinite slaps to the face

Music Meister Badge

"You've got the touch! You've got the power!"

There exists that one song—the one that can pull you up from the deepest depths and take you into the next dimension. It's the song that is there for you when you need it the most. Music and emotions are almost too hard to separate, and it's that passion that hooks right into the geek soul. Whether it's a progressive rock ballad about alien abduction, a classic folk song about interstellar shenanigans, or a clever parody filled with wordplay, geeky music can do just about anything. Be excellent to each other.

Music Styles of the Geeky Persuasion

There is a stunning variety of music specifically for geek ears. Here are but a few of the most popular genres.

geeky folk

parody

nerdcore

wizard rock

anything by Rush

How Generally Geeky is this Song?

It's important to keep track of any mention of these classic geek subjects.

- wizards
- elves
- robots
- zombies
- dinosaurs
- homicidal AIs
- science (especially of the weird variety)
- Boba Fett

* Extra points for a song about hobbits sung by Spock

My Own Perfect Geek Playlist

Fill in the mixtape label with your ideal geek playlist.

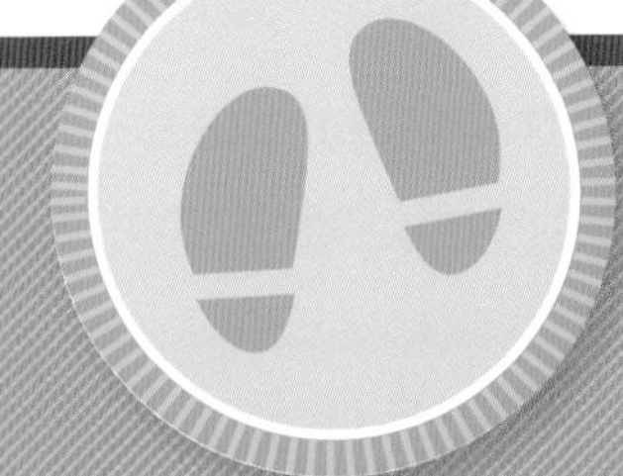

Victory Dance Choreography Badge

"You can dance if you want to."

If you won't celebrate yourself, who will? Wins can be depressingly few and far between, so when you get one, you have to let your body move to the rhythm. Who cares who's watching? It's not for them: It's for the strong geek you know yourself to be. Let that power ballad blast through to the very heavens themselves—for today you won.

Victory Dance Moves

You can create your own unique victory dance by mixing and matching some of the following simple moves.

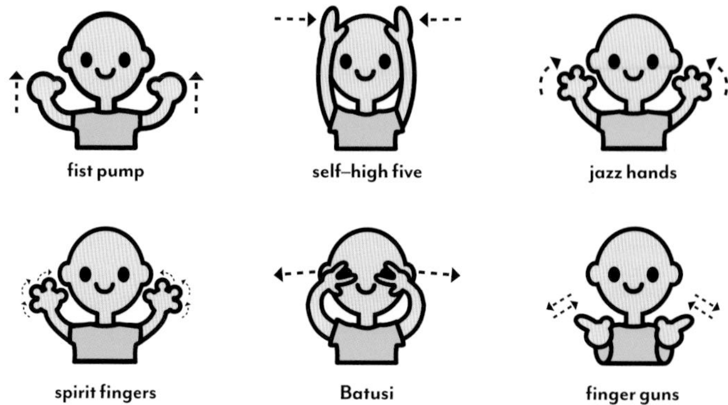

Notable Nerds Who Dance

Mostly to their own beat.

- Napoleon Dynamite
- Steve Urkel
- Carlton Banks
- Mary Catherine Gallagher
- Pee-wee Herman
- Ed Grimley
- Conan O'Brien
- Bill Nye
- Leslie Hall

Personal Victories Chart

Keep a list of your victories and which level of celebration would be appropriate for each. Fill in the stars to rate your wins!

....
☆☆☆☆☆

....
☆☆☆☆☆

....
☆☆☆☆☆

....
☆☆☆☆☆

....
☆☆☆☆☆

(one star = a pat on the back)

(five stars = *dance party!!!*)

Weirdness Wizardry Badge

"Surely you can't be serious."

There are times when you have to swerve into the skid. Own it. Yeah, you may be odd. Strange. Don't fit in. But you've always known that, and it's time for you to realize how amazing that makes you. Geeks are on a different wavelength than most of the world, so we are attuned to hidden beauty and joy that others will never see. Geeks are the lucky ones.

Benefits to Being Silly for Silly's Sake

There can be rhyme in having no reason.

- It's hard to stay stressed when making a funny face.
- It's the opposite of bureaucracy.
- Your brain needs the stretch.
- Sometimes a clown nose is the perfect accessory.
- You're never going to catch Bigfoot with sense or sensibility.

The Beauty of Not Giving a Crap What Anyone Thinks

A few reminders to keep in mind whenever you start worrying about what other people think.

- They don't know you.
- You don't have to please everyone. (Especially jackasses.)
- You can put up a "No Unwanted Visitors" sign in your mind whenever you want.
- Keep moving and leave critical voices to eddy in your wake.
- You know you are wonderful. Nothing can change that.

Stranger in a Predictable Land

Here are some ideas for everyday oddity. Bring some unpredictable joy into the world. Be weird!

Purposely wear mismatched socks.

Keep singing along to the radio in your car even when someone pulls up next to you.

Eat everything at one meal with your fingers (extra points for soup).

Make up a song about your pets. Or the squirrel that watches you from your window.

Surprise glitter!*

* WARNING: Deploy only if you're ready to find glitter everywhere for the year. It's not called the herpes of the craft world for nothing.

In Conclusion

So how are your geek levels now? All charged up and ready for more? Feel that enthusiam and energy just waiting for you to tap into it? You're going to earn all those badges. I know you will, because you are a good geek.

There are so many ways to be a geek, but being a good geek is simple.

Love what you love.
Be what you love.
Share what you love.

You do that, and you are going to be all right.

BADGE TRACKERS

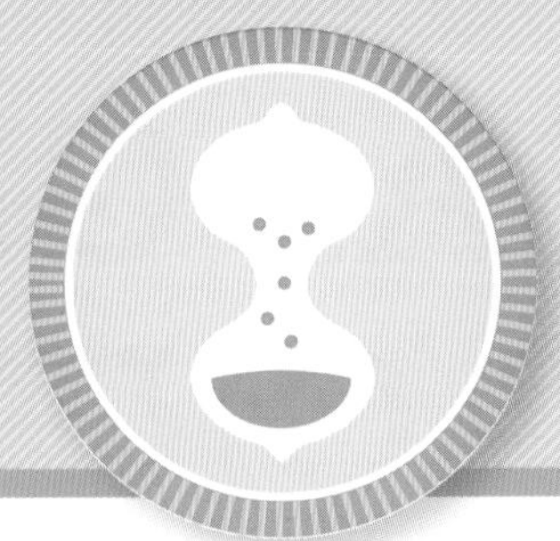

Time and Time Again Badge

- ❑ read "Time Travel Possibilities"
- ❑ thought about "Reasons for Time Travel"
- ❑ studied "Paradox Avoidance Chart"
- ❑ finished "Personal Time Travel Plan"

NOTES:

"No matter where you go, there you are."

—**BUCKAROO BANZAI,**
The Adventures of Buckaroo Banzai Across the 8th Dimension

Awkardness Adept Badge

- ❏ did "Awkward Level Check"
- ❏ studied "Helpful Eye Contact Chart"
- ❏ finished "The Art of Artlessness"

NOTES:

"I, myself, am strange and unusual."

—**LYDIA DEETZ,** *Beetlejuice*

Comrades in Arms Badge

- ❑ learned "Ways to Describe a Geektastic Relationship"
- ❑ used the "Possible Interactions Database"
- ❑ finished "Build Your Party"

NOTES:

"I have been—and always shall be—your friend."

- **SPOCK,** *Star Trek II: The Wrath of Khan*

Health Bar Awareness Badge

- ❏ learned about "Ways Your Geekery Will Try to Kill You"
- ❏ asked self "Have You Ever Suffered From... ?"
- ❏ calculated if "This All-Nighter Is Worth It"
- ❏ programmed my "Self-Destruct Override Sequence"

NOTES:

....

....

....

....

....

....

"The spice must flow."

- **BARON HARKONNEN**, *Dune*

Culture Code Badge

❑ answered your "Geeky Choices"
❑ studied "How to Watch a Twilight Zone Marathon"
❑ learned some "Geeky Life Mottos (and Their Meanings)"
❑ filled out "What Did We Learn Today?"

NOTES:

"I find your lack of faith disturbing."

- **DARTH VADER,** *Star Wars: Episode IV - A New Hope*

Your Own Worst Enemy Badge

- ❑ on the watch for "Evil Twin Signs"
- ❑ constantly in the midst of "Evil Twin Spotting"
- ❑ answered (and hid!) my "Fail-Safe Questions"

NOTES:

"Good. Bad. I'm the guy with the gun."

- **ASH,** *Army of Darkness*

Call to Adventure Badge

- ❑ wrote down "My Geeky Firsts"
- ❑ studied the "Life Cycle of a Geeky Love"
- ❑ am open to "Scouting Ahead"

NOTES:

"Roads? Where we're going, we don't need roads."

- **DR. EMMETT BROWN,** *Back to the Future*

Origin Story Badge

❏ studied "A Collection of Possible Origins"

❏ completed "A Repository of Creation"

❏ wrote "The Me. The Myth. The Legend."

NOTES:

"With great power comes great responsibility."

- **UNCLE BEN,** *various incarnations of the Spider-Man origin story*

Joined the Party Badge

❏ filled out "My First Fandom"

❏ perused the "Assorted Relevant Charts"

❏ drew "My First Fandom Portrait"

NOTES:

"It's alive!"

- **DR. HENRY FRANKENSTEIN,** *Frankenstein*

Found Your Voice Badge

❏ completed "Geeky Source Material"

❏ studied "Feeding the Machine"

❏ finished "Hit Record and Save"

NOTES:

"You've always had the power my dear, you just had to learn it for yourself."

- **GLINDA,** *The Wizard of Oz*

Caffeine Command Badge

- ❏ used "Tested and Approved Energy Sources"
- ❏ followed "Artificial Energy Limitations"
- ❏ filled out "Identifying Energy Sucks"

NOTES:

"Damn good coffee! And hot!"

- **AGENT DALE COOPER,** *Twin Peaks*

Plot Pathfinder Badge

❑ completed "Quest Journal"

❑ read "The Dos and Don'ts of Successful Narrative Navigation"

❑ finished "Is This Trip Necessary?"

NOTES:

"Trust me. I'm the Doctor."

- DOCTOR WHO

Top Ten Badge

- ❑ read "Top Ten Ways Top Ten Lists are the Best"
- ❑ read "Top Ten Ways Top Ten Lists are the Worst"
- ❑ read "Top Ten Reasons for Top Ten Lists"
- ❑ read "Top Six Reasons It's Usually a Top Ten List"
- ❑ finished "Overlooked Rankings"

NOTES:

"You're the best around. Nothing's ever gonna keep you down."

- from the song "You're the Best," The Karate Kid

Constant Collector Badge

- ❏ perused "Collectible Desirability and Value Perception Chart"
- ❏ thought about "So Many Possible Collectibles!"
- ❏ wrote "A History of My Collection"

NOTES:

"Gotta catch 'em all!"

- slogan of all dedicated Pokémon trainers

Outrageous Rage Badge

- ❏ understood "The Art of Outsized Anger Maintenance"
- ❏ read "The Geek Serenity Meditation"
- ❏ filled out "Geek Serenity in Action"
- ❏ completed "My Personal Rage Gauge"

NOTES:

"That's my secret, Captain: I'm always angry."

- **BRUCE BANNER,** *The Avengers*

Game Master Badge

- ❑ read "Reasons to Love Board Games"
- ❑ checked "How to Recognize the Game Master Inside"
- ❑ finished "Known Friendship Enders: Is Winning Worth It?"

NOTES:

"Greetings, programs!"

- **KEVIN FLYNN,** *Tron*

Eternal Student Badge

- ❑ studied "Common Objects of Adoration"
- ❑ learned "How to Deal with Your Unread Books"
- ❑ checked off "Common Signs You Never Stop Learning"

NOTES:

"You're gonna need a bigger boat."

- **CHIEF BRODY,** *Jaws*

Speak the Language Badge

❏ did "Check Your Fictional Language Expertise"

❏ giggled at "A Grawlix of Fantastic Swears"

❏ filled in "Get to Know Your Fictional Languages"

NOTES:

"So say we all."

- concluding ceremonial response, Battlestar Galactica

Officially Obsessed Badge

- ❏ looked at "Percentage of Brain Activity Devoted to Obsession"
- ❏ learned "The Care and Feeding of An Obsession"
- ❏ competed "The Obsession Cycle"
- ❏ cataloged "What Are Your Obsessions and Their First Sparks"

NOTES:

"I've got a bad feeling about this..."

- repeated throughout Star Wars franchise (and beyond)

Receiving on All Frequencies Badge

- ❑ followed "How to Stay Tuned In to a Conversation"
- ❑ found out about "Recognizing Your Own Interface"
- ❑ finished "Open Your Hailing Channels"

NOTES:

"As you wish."

- **WESTLEY,** *The Princess Bride*

Nostalgia Navigation Badge

- ❏ completed "Facing the Past"
- ❏ understood "Nostalgia Overload Warning Signs"
- ❏ filled out "Nostalgia Hacks"

NOTES: ....

....

....

....

....

....

....

....

....

....

"Valar Morghulis."

- **ARYA STARK (AMONG OTHERS),** *A Song of Ice and Fire/Game of Thrones*

Extroverted Inversion Badge

- ❏ checked "Geeking Out with Others"
- ❏ studied "Charging Station"
- ❏ reviewed "Pushing Your Boundaries"

NOTES:

"Wait till they get a load of me!"

- **THE JOKER,** *Batman (1989)*

Persona Production Badge

❏ read "The Benefits of a Virtual Avatar"

❏ cut and pasted the "Offline Avatar Maker"

❏ finished "Believe It or Not, It's Just Me"

NOTES:

"We are what we pretend to be, so we must be careful about what we pretend to be."

- **KURT VONNEGUT,** *from the introduction of his novel Mother Night*

Awesomeness Ambassador Badge

- ❏ studied "How to Recognize You've Found the Awesome"
- ❏ learned "Warning Signs of Disengagement"
- ❏ perused "How an Awesome Infection Spreads"
- ❏ completed "A Cold Call Script for Awesome"

NOTES:

"I've seen things you people wouldn't believe."

- **ROY BATTY,** *Blade Runner*

Welcoming Committee Badge

- ❑ understood "Open the Doors Wide!"
- ❑ viewed "Fool-Proof Geek Detection Chart"
- ❑ filled out "A Geek Starter Kit"

NOTES:

"Well, welcome home to Happiness Hotel..."

- **MANAGEMENT OF THE HAPPINESS HOTEL,** *The Great Muppet Caper*

Lending Library Badge

- ❑ learned about "A Stark Truth"
- ❑ read "Why Lend Books?"
- ❑ completed "Create Your Own Book Plates"

NOTES:

"It's a moral imperative."

- **CHRIS KNIGHT,** *Real Genius*

Mighty Mentor Badge

- ❑ studied "Classic Mentor Archetypes"
- ❑ learned "How to be a Mentor"
- ❑ finished "Your Repository of Enlightenment"

NOTES:

"Do not meddle in the affairs of wizards."

- **GILDOR INGLORION,** *The Fellowship of the Ring*

Disaster Preparedness Badge

- ❑ got ready for "Are You Ready?"
- ❑ appreciated "Being in the Now"
- ❑ assembled "My Apocalyptic Dream Team"

NOTES:

"Can't we just get beyond Thunderdome?"

- CROW AND TOM SERVO (WITH AN UNCOOPERATIVE MIKE),
MST3k Episode 706 - Laserblast

Advanced Armor Badge

- ❏ reviewed "T-Shirt Totality Chart"
- ❏ studied "Hoodie: All-Purpose Awesome"
- ❏ designed "My Power Suit"

NOTES:

"Your clothes. Give them to me. Now."

- **TERMINATOR,** *The Terminator*

Keeper of Traditions Badge

- ❏ learned "Classic Geek Traditions"
- ❏ wrote "My Custom List of Customs"
- ❏ created "That New, Old-Time Tradition!"

NOTES:

"Stay awhile and listen."

- **DECKARD CAIN,** *Diablo*

Fan Fiction Finesse Badge

- ❏ figured out "Your Fan Fiction Level"
- ❏ found out about "The Health Benefits of Fan Fiction"
- ❏ used "The Perfect Mary Sue or Gary Stu Generator"

NOTES:

"Make it so."

- **CAPTAIN JEAN-LUC PICARD,** *Star Trek: The Next Generation*

Crafty Crafter Badge

- ❏ discovered "So Many Crafty Possibilities"
- ❏ read "The Art of Geekcraft"
- ❏ finished "What Kind of Craft Is For Me?"

NOTES:

"They've gone to plaid!"

- **BARF,** *Spaceballs*

Command Center Badge

- ❑ tried out "Quick Ways to Geekify Your Room"
- ❑ was inspired by "Home is Where Your Laser Cannon Is"
- ❑ completed "What Headquarters Style Fits You the Best?"

NOTES:

"To infinity... and beyond!"

- **BUZZ LIGHTYEAR,** *Toy Story*

Inky Fingers Badge

- ❏ checked "Are You a Fan of Fan Art?"
- ❏ read "Choose Your Instrument"
- ❏ drew "My First Fan Art"

NOTES:

"See You Space Cowboy..."

- **MOST END TITLE CARDS,** *Cowboy Bebop*

Tinker/Hacker/Fixer Badge

- ❏ perused "A Hacker Mind-Set"
- ❏ studied "A Tinkerer's Tool Kit"
- ❏ understood "Just Because You Can Doesn't Mean You Should"

NOTES:

"Never give up. Never surrender."

- **JASON NESMITH,** *Galaxy Quest*

Cosplay Commando Badge

- ❑ read "I'm Pulling the Wig Down From the Shelf"
- ❑ was inspired by "Variations on a Theme"
- ❑ answered "Who Do You Want to Be?"

NOTES:

"Don't dream it. Be it."

- **DR. FRANK-N-FURTER,** *The Rocky Horror Picture Show*

Creative Cookery Badge

- ❑ studied "Famous Fictional Foods"
- ❑ found "Traditional Gaming Snacks"
- ❑ read "Don't Forget to Hydrate"

NOTES:

"The snozzberries taste like snozzberries."

- **WILLY WONKA,** *Willy Wonka & the Chocolate Factory*

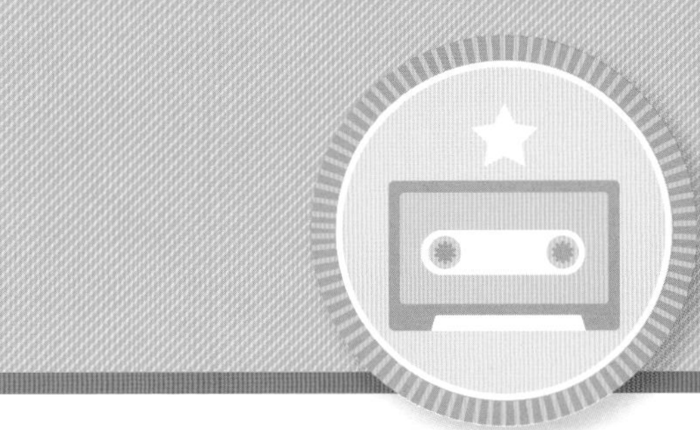

Music Meister Badge

❏ learned "Music Styles of the Geeky Persuasion"

❏ discovered "How Generally Geeky is this Song?"

❏ created "My Own Perfect Geek Playlist"

NOTES:

"You've got the Touch! You've got the Power!"

- **FROM THE SONG "THE TOUCH,"** *The Transformers: The Movie*

Victory Dance Choreography Badge

❑ designed "Victory Dance Moves"

❑ studied "Notable Nerds Who Dance"

❑ completed the "Personal Victories Chart"

NOTES:

"You can dance if you want to."

- lyrics from "The Safety Dance," by Men Without Hats

Weirdness Wizardry Badge

- ❑ perused Benefits to "Being Silly for Silly's Sake"
- ❑ read "The Beauty of Not Giving a Crap What Anyone Thinks"
- ❑ finished "Stranger in a Predictable Land"

NOTES:

"Surely you can't be serious."

- **TED STRIKER,** *Airplane*

APPENDIX A:

SIGNS FOR THE TRAVELING GEEK

Just like the Depression-era hoboes often used a code of quick sketches and marks to warn their fellow travelers of any dangers up ahead on the road, so should geeks start to employ our own pictorial language to help each other out in the sometimes cold and not-always nerd-friendly world. Here are just a few useful symbols to get you started, but please feel free to create some of your own as well—there are so many important and particularly geeky things that need to be communicated!

Nerd spoken here.

Good reading spot.

Look for Easter eggs

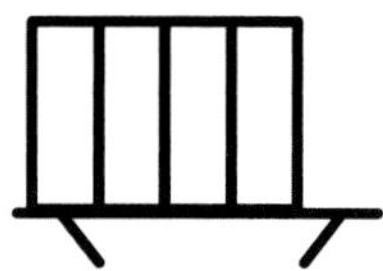

Bookshelf almost full.

Spoiler alert!

Evil DM.

Need alone time.

Sarcasm warning.

Possible awkward.

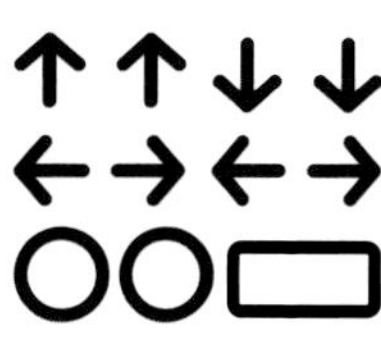

Cheat code available

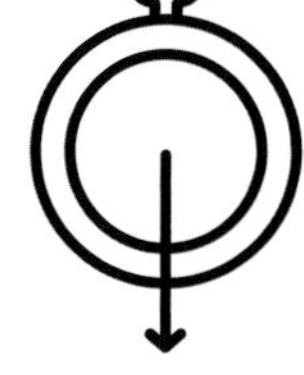

Time sink ahead.

Cancellation imminent.

APPENDIX B:
GEEK SECRETS

Well, you've made it to the end of the book. I can tell you're serious about your geek studies. You're now ready for the deepest and darkest secrets. Prepare yourself, seeker.

- Extra credit is not always worth it.
- Some shows deserved to be cancelled.
- That movie you loved as a kid just doesn't hold up. At all.
- You can spend too much time plugged in.
- Star Wars and Star Trek are equally as good.
- But the most important secret of all is this: It's *all* subjective. Even this list. And that's not just ok; that's amazing. Because that means it's all up to you: what you like, what you love, what you create. Whatever kind of geek you want to be is entirely up to you. And I know you can handle it. Go forth and be awesome!

INDEX

More Great Titles from HOW Books

OMG! I Forgot the Card

By Claudean Wheeler & Scott Francis

Have you ever waited until the last minute to buy a card, or realized you completely forgot to buy one altogether? Never find yourself without a proper greeting again with this convenient book of ready-to-fold-and-mail greeting cards. Included are holiday cards, birthday cards, get well cards and much more.

Toy Confidential

By Aled Lewis

With more pop culture references than you can shake an Ewok at, *Toy Confidential* offers a return to childhood—only with better jokes. Ever wanted to see *Jurassic Park* only with skateboards? How about *Scarface* reenacted by cute little pug puppies? Check and check. Grow up? Never!

The Book of Rules

By Joshua Belter

Which way should the toilet paper be dispensed from the roll? Who goes first at an intersection in a grocery store? What is the proper placement of ketchup on a plate? When is it appropriate to dress your pet in clothes that match your own? If you've ever wondered about the answers to these vital questions, this is the book for you.

Find these books and many others at MyDesignShop.com or your local bookstore.

For more news, tips and articles, follow us at **Twitter.com/HOWbrand**

For behind-the-scenes information and special offers, become a fan at **Facebook.com/HOWmagazine**

For visual inspiration, follow us at **Pinterest.com/HOWbrand**

SPECIAL OFFER FROM HOW BOOKS!

You can get 15% off your entire order at MyDesignShop.com! All you have to do is go to **www.howdesign.com/howbooks-offer** and sign up for our free e-newsletter on graphic design. You'll also get a free digital download of HOW magazine.

10
!@%#$